T0162817

# BETWEEN

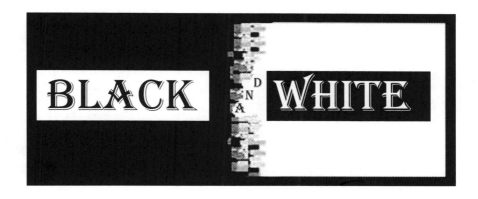

BLACK aND WHITE

Leon Vaughn Gilchrist, Jr.
Phillip Martin Williamson
Alan H. Smith

authorHOUSE®

*AuthorHouse*™
*1663 Liberty Drive*
*Bloomington, IN 47403*
*www.authorhouse.com*
*Phone: 1-800-839-8640*

© *2012 by Leon Vaughn Gilchrist, Jr., Phillip Martin Williamson and Alan H. Smith. All rights reserved.*

*No part of this book may be reproduced, stored in a retrieval system, or transmitted by any means without the written permission of the author.*

*Published by AuthorHouse    05/04/2012*

*ISBN: 978-1-4685-6889-9 (sc)*
*ISBN: 978-1-4685-6888-2 (e)*

*Any people depicted in stock imagery provided by Thinkstock are models, and such images are being used for illustrative purposes only.*
*Certain stock imagery © Thinkstock.*

*This book is printed on acid-free paper.*

*Because of the dynamic nature of the Internet, any web addresses or links contained in this book may have changed since publication and may no longer be valid. The views expressed in this work are solely those of the author and do not necessarily reflect the views of the publisher, and the publisher hereby disclaims any responsibility for them.*

# CONTENTS

# EASYInk is Just Write

# PREFACE

L ife requires our participation in the determination of how our individual lives will unfold. The participation will either be active or inactive. Active participation involves the engagement of choosing a defining direction and working to make life choices that agree with the personally defined direction. Inactive participation, on the other hand, is a passive existence through life which results from not having a defined direction in which to live. The hope of finding satisfaction can only exist when active participation is embarked upon.

# CHAPTER 1

# Grey's Dilemma

Hello—my name is George Grey. My friends call me Grey. I have a nice paying job, a couple of nice cars, a wife and two kids. I, along with my loving family, attend Middle Valley Missionary Baptist Church in Northern New Jersey. As faithful members of Miss Baptist, as we affectionately refer to our church, my wife, children and I serve and participate in various church activities up to and including, of course, missionary ministries. I'm well liked at church, in my community and on my job. I'm a pretty stable, calm thinker of a man. I have investments, just a few dollars in the stock market, but I don't play the market. I buy and sell conservatively, with as little risk as possible. I enjoy sleeping at night and I have managed to keep my hair over many years of investing and corrections in the market.

My salary is all the money that comes into the house. Once in a while I bet on a horse in the Derby. Not too much though. If I lose a little I don't mind. It's all in good fun. But, I bet small, so I never win big. I make it all work financially because I'm a conservative spender and really good at saving money. All in all our needs and wants are met. By no stretch of the imagination am I wealthy, but my family in no way is lacking for anything they need. Despite what might sound like a good life, though, I'm anything but happy. I'm a man who, despite the human and material treasures in his life, feels a deep emptiness: an emptiness that I believe results from being predictable and living a predictable life, where all that I do and have done is expected and safe.

At this point, I believe that planning ahead, making sure that all is in place, so that things don't go awry, is good. Poor planning or even worse, no planning is never a good thing. But it seems that plans that are turned into script leave no room for flexibility.

Recently, I received the news of a good friend of mine who suddenly passed away. His name was Hector Santiago. Hector lived freely and in his own way. He liked doing new and different things and going to new and different places. He wasn't driven by fear or the expectations of others. Hector did what Hector wanted to do.

Several years back when we were in our mid-twenties, it seems like a lifetime ago now, I remember Hector telling me that he joined the military when he was eighteen years old. He told me that he simply woke up one morning with the idea of joining the military and right after eating breakfast, that arbitrary morning in the eighteenth year of his life, he marched down to the army recruiting office and joined. I was amazed, but it wasn't the fact that he joined that was so amazing. It was the fact that he made a life altering decision on the spur of the moment. Losing Hector was a hard blow. He added a great deal to my life.

We met under tense and quite unusual circumstances at a chicken place across from my church. The funny thing is that Hector never viewed the conditions of our meeting quite the way I did. Every time I told the story he always claimed that I grossly exaggerated what happened that day. For our twenty five or so year friendship, though, we remained loyal to agree to disagree on the point.

Moments before hearing the news of his death I was preoccupied with feeling unfulfilled. It was a feeling of what I would think a slow and dreadful death would be. I was trying to figure out a solution to save my life, a life of black clouds and inclement weather, in order to experience a world of rays of sunshine beaming through the clouds. I sat in my den on my Lazy Boy chair pensively staring out into the dimly lit space hoping that answers and solutions to my deepening discontentment would somehow be revealed. Lost in my thoughts, I was startled back to reality by my wife, Paula, who was standing over me gently nudging my shoulder and handing me the phone.

Looking up toward her, I mouthed, "Who is it?"

With a sick look on her face she mouthed back, "Hazel." Hazel was Hector's wife.

With an eerie feeling in the pit of my stomach, I put the phone to my ear and spoke, "Hello?"

I heard Hazel draw a deep breath, then whisper, "George—this is Hazel." After a pause she continued, "George, Hector—died last night." I was taken totally off guard, but managed to compose myself. In as much pain as anyone could imagine, Hazel went on, "George—it was a drunk driver: a drunk driver George." She paused again to compose herself. I heard quiet sobbing. After drawing another deep breath and exhaling, she continued, "George, my Hector is gone. He's gone George. I understand now George. Tomorrow is not promised. Hector always said that George. He knew that all we have is the moment we're in. I have to go now George. I just wanted to be the one to tell you. I'll talk to you and Paula later." We each said our goodbyes and hung up. I was numb. I didn't know how to feel. I didn't know what to feel. Paula joined me on the Lazy Boy where we reclined together for about a half an hour in silence. It was good having Paula near me.

The next day I couldn't get Hazel's words out of my mind.

"Now I understand George. Tomorrow is not promised. Hector always said that George." Hazel was right. Hector never looked at tomorrow as a guarantee and for that reason he lived his life more in the moment than in a tomorrow that might not come. Hector lived what always seemed to me as being a no holds barred style of life.

Although there were times I found myself entertaining having Hector's life, in all honesty, I can't say that I ever truly desired it. It was always a bit too risky and irresponsible for me, but even having always felt that way, there was also an alluring quality about it. Hector lived to satisfy Hector and what Hector held to be important. I would say that what others thought of him didn't matter. If he wanted to do something but his parents, wife, friends or what was common thought were not in agreement, he'd do it if he felt that it would serve his purpose. There was a freedom in the way Hector lived.

The way I live, on the other hand, is very different and in many ways is like living as an inmate of a personally crafted and constructed prison where the no-risk and confrontation-avoiding parts of me serve as the warden. My prison is full of The American Dream amenities but as time marches on restlessness grows inside me, pushing me into a quandary. Have I been living The American Dream at the expense of my freedom? Have I been living with no real identified purpose? So many discontenting questions clutter my mind.

The day of Hector's funeral came fast. It was on a Saturday: a complete week from the day of his untimely death. My wife and I attended the funeral. Among the other mourners in attendance were two of my childhood friends of whom I hadn't seen for a couple of years, Rayford Jones and Clarence Davenport. We all knew Hector but I had the closest relationship with him. Because I accepted a request earlier in the week, I was a bit on edge. A few days after Hazel had called telling me of Hector's demise, she called back asking if I would share a few words at the funeral.

I told her I would. How could I not? As I sat nervously awaiting my time to speak, I reminisced over the varied experiences I had with Hector: experiences I know I wouldn't have had except by Hector's initiation and invitation. When the time came for me to share my words, I walked to the microphone and spoke from my heart.

After sharing my few words about Hector I left the pulpit and returned to my seat. Following the final prayer, the church emptied: those of us who were in attendance quietly and respectfully headed to our automobiles. One behind the other, we aligned our vehicles to form a procession to the cemetery. After giving our final respects at the grave site we returned to the church for a bitter sweet repast: bitter simply due to the occasion, but sweet due to the familiar faces that only funerals and weddings seem to have the power to gather. After leaving the church Paula and I went home. Rayford and Clarence followed us there. While my friends and I sat on the porch, Paula went inside to finish cooking. She wanted to take some food to Hazel the next day.

There on my porch, that late Saturday autumn evening, I sat with my two closest friends from childhood. We didn't say much at first. We just sat and looked out at the neighborhood comfortably enjoying the quiet pedestrian traffic and the beautiful weather. After a while Paula brought out a tray with three tall glasses of iced tea.

"Thanks babe," I told her, then gave her a little pat on her behind.

With a school-girl smile, she moved out of range and heading back inside told me, in an adorable tone, "You better keep those hands to yourself Mister, that is, if you know what's good for you." We all let out a good laugh as the door closed behind her.

With a satisfied smile on his face, Clarence looked at me while nodding his head and said, "Man, I need to get you and Paula to speak at one of my church's marriage seminars."

Still staring out from the porch, toothpick in his mouth and his feet propped up on the wood railing of my porch, Rayford added, "Yeah, y'all still got it—huh George? Man, alot of dudes would love to have your life." Uncontrollably my mood and demeanor changed. My spirit plummeted. I knew Rayford didn't notice because he hadn't taken his eyes from his street directed gaze, but out of the corner of my eye I saw that Clarence had noticed and had turned his head toward me.

Clueless, Rayford continued staring up and down the street.

Clarence, however, with his eyes fixed on me finally decided to break his silence, "What's going on in that head of yours Grey? Something made you flip from on to off."

I answered, "Rayford said a lot of guys would love to have my life." I paused and laughed in my most self-mocking tone then I continued, "If people knew what my life was really like they wouldn't want it. People like action and adventure. My life has neither." I withdrew for a moment then, running my hand down over my face, I collected myself and spoke again, "I'm not ready to die."

Clarence responded, "Come on George, who really is ready to die? God knows this is the only existence we really know and that death by comparison is a huge unknown."

With a turned up face I responded, "No, I don't mean it like that."

Confused, Clarence asked, "Then what do you mean?"

Feeling the all too familiar burden of my dilemma creeping up on me, I tried to explain, "Hector is gone. Nobody saw it coming, but he's gone. What if I die tonight? I won't even be a blip on the radar."

Unchanged in posture Rayford calmly spoke again, "Yo—you got one life to live, so live it good, then call it a life." My frustration progressed to anger and to be honest—jealousy.

"Yeah, I guess that's how a big time city roller like you got it goin' on—huh Rayford? Everything you touch turns to a wild, heart-pumping, solid gold adventure. Well I ain't got it quite like that Rayford! I'm not like you and Hector."

After blurting that out, both Rayford and Clarence turned to me with looks that communicated their total confusion over what had just happened. Rayford had even taken his feet down from the railing and turned to me as he removed the toothpick from his mouth. Elbows on my spread knees, I hung my head. Cradled in my hands I held my forehead. I was embarrassed and my head hurt. Not moving from my pose I drew a deep breath and as I exhaled I spoke again, "I'm sorry. I'm just in a bad way. I don't know what I'm supposed to do. I just don't know what I'm supposed to be doing."

# CHAPTER 2

# The Stranger in the Woods

It was the first day of my third grade year. I walked to school by myself. There were other kids with whom I could have walked, but I didn't want any company. I just wanted to be alone for the last moments before the start of another school year.

To get the most out of my walk, and make it last, I decided to take the long way to school. The long way happened to be through the woods along the creek. The view of the creek against the woods always made me feel good and it didn't fail me on that hot September morning. Though it was hot, there was a nice breeze blowing and once I got to the creek, under all the trees, it was actually cool. I was whistling as I walked along the raised embankment of the creek. Occasionally, I looked down into the creek and along its muddy and grassy banks. My hope was to see something moving. A week earlier I caught a salamander. I have always been interested in discovering animal-life along the creek.

Startled by the sound of a snapped twig, I abruptly paused, crouched down and turned in the direction of the sound. I envisioned myself as an Indian scout. Indians, as I had come to know from television westerns, always fascinated me. Crouched down with one knee on the ground and the other pointing upwards, I watched for the slightest movement in the near distance. Just as I was about to dismiss the sound caused by a bird or a squirrel, I saw something move just beyond the bend of the creek in front of me. It was a person. I was sure. I quietly crept closer. Pushing the branches of a bush to one side I saw a boy in the clearing. He was collecting twigs, branches and logs. I moved to find a more comfortable position when out of nowhere a fair amount of gaseous matter involuntarily escaped from under me. It was loud. I closed my eyes and held my breath, hoping that somehow the noise from this most unfortunate and untimely occurrence would go unnoticed.

Eyes still closed and continuing to hold my breath, I heard these words, "If you think I can't see you, you're wrong. I see you and even if I didn't see you, I definitely heard you. Yep, I smell you too. You might as well come out and face me like a man." I opened my eyes, exhaled and walked into the clearing where I stood waiting for the stranger to make the next move. He spoke again, "Well don't just stand there looking stupid. We already know you were the one who farted."

Indignantly I replied, "I did not. I passed gas."

"No, a refined lady passes gas. You just plain farted. Now stop avoiding the truth and make yourself useful and help me collect some tree branches."

A bit confused I asked, "Why, wha . . . what are you doing?"

The stranger answered, "I'm making a fort. I've got rope, a hammer and some nails. All I need now is wood."

Realizing what time it was getting to be, I told the stranger that I couldn't help him at the moment because I had to get to school.

He replied, "Well I'm supposed to be in school too, but first things first. I have a fort to build. You got one life to live, so live it good then call it a life. That's what my uncle always says." Although I wanted to help with the fort, I didn't want to risk getting in trouble living my life "good."

It didn't quite add up to me how doing something wrong could equate to living well. As far as I was concerned avoiding trouble was the way to live a good life.

With a sort of sheepish look on my face, I broke the news to the stranger, "I'm going to school, but I'll come back when school is out and if you're still here, I'll help you."

Resuming his wood collecting, the stranger simply said, "Do whatcha gotta do. Every man rows his own boat. You see what I'm sayin'?" I had never met anyone like this before. In a way he was rude, but he didn't really offend me. To tell the truth, I thought he was just a real honest kind of kid. There was something about him I really liked.

As I turned to leave, he blurted out, "You got a name? Mine's Jones, Rayford Jones, like double O seven." With that he let out a series of laughs: deep, hearty laughs that stirred me to laugh. In the midst of me laughing, I managed to give him my name.

"George Grey," I said, pointing to my chest using my thumb.

Rayford looked at me and with a nodding of his head and a cool smile said, "Imma call you Grey. Yeah, I like that. It fits you." Knowing I would barely make it to school on time, I left the clearing with Rayford hard at work on his fort.

With a peculiar joy I tilted my head to the side and yelled out, "I'll see you later Rayford Jones!" as I ran to school.

# CHAPTER 3

# *Ordained*

I couldn't believe that I made it to school right at the bell. I took my seat sweating. I looked around the classroom and smiled and waved to some classmates I hadn't seen since school let out for the summer. Standing in front of the class was a person I didn't recognize.

"Hello class, my name is Miss Delilah Cunningham. I will be your teacher this year. Most of you were probably expecting Mrs. Johnston, but she won't be with us this year." Mrs. Johnston was our second grade teacher but before we broke for summer, we were told that she was going to be our third grade teacher as well.

From behind the room a voice asked, "Where is Mrs. Johnston? Why isn't she going to be our teacher?" Mrs. Cunningham was younger and much prettier than Mrs. Johnston, but we loved Mrs. Johnston. She was like family and she knew how to teach us. She really knew how to make learning fun.

In answer to the question and quite matter-of-fact, I might add, Mrs. Cunningham replied, "I don't know. They didn't tell me." I guess seeing no need to continue along this subject path, Mrs. Cunningham abruptly changed the subject. "I need to take attendance so listen for your name. When I call your name raise your hand and say—present." Mrs. Cunningham was clearly an "About-the-Business" type of teacher. She put a pair of old lady spectacles on and before long she started her roll call.

As each student's name was called it was clear Mrs. Cunningham's instructions were heard and understood. I was waiting to hear my name so I could respond in kind.

"George Grey."

I raised my hand and in my clearest voice, I responded, "Present."

"Clarence Davenport."

Hand raised, Clarence responded, "Blessed by God and present." There were chuckles across the room. Stoic, Mrs. Cunningham looked over the top rim of her glasses, as if to etch Clarence's face into her memory.

She looked back down at her roll sheet, but before continuing, void of any real emotion and with no eye contact with the class stated, "I trust we won't have any other departures from the instructions given." Satisfied that her sentiment was communicated, Mrs. Cunningham continued. The next several students whose names were called returned to the compliance that had existed before Clarence's name was called.

When she called the next name, "Rayford Jones," I popped my head up. Mrs. Cunningham paused. She then repeated the name, "Rayford Jones." She whispered, "absent," and continued. Once the attendance had been taken, Mrs. Cunningham instructed us to take our science books out. They were already in our desks. She told us to turn to Chapter 1 and there she began to teach us about evolution. I'm usually interested in science, but science was the furthest thing from my mind. I was still smiling about Rayford being in my class and thinking about the fort.

As Mrs. Cunningham was talking about evolution her attention became fixed on Clarence.

"Mr. Davenport, what is it that you have hidden behind your science book? It better not be anything inappropriate or offensive." Clarence didn't answer. Mrs. Cunningham walked over and stood over his desk. "Give it to me," she demanded as she stretched out her hand to receive what Clarence was hiding. As Clarence handed the material to Mrs. Cunningham, a very puzzled look came over her face. "Why on earth, Mr. Davenport, are you reading the Bible in class? Does this look like church to you?"

"No mam," answered Clarence.

"Then why are you reading it Mr. Davenport?"

Not intimidated by Mrs. Cunningham's authority over him, Clarence respectfully replied, "Mam—I don't believe in evolution and I think it displeases God, so I decided to please God by reading his Word until you were done talking about evolution."

Clearly unimpressed Mrs. Cunningham said, "Go to the office and tell the principal that you want to read your bible in class. Mr. Grey—escort Mr. Davenport to the office and promptly return."

Clarence and I walked slowly to the office. I knew Clarence, but not that well.

Looking straight ahead as we walked I said to Clarence, "Mrs. Cunningham's kinda mean isn't she?"

A bit distant Clarence responded, "Man, I miss Mrs. Johnston. There's no way she would have sent me to the principal's office for reading the Bible." In our short time talking as we walked to the office, I got to know Clarence better than I did all the previous years we were in class together. In that short walk I gained a respect for him that was unlike any respect I had for any other kid.

When I got back to class, I couldn't believe my eyes. Jones, Rayford Jones was sitting in class. For Mrs. Cunningham to allow him in class he had to have come from the office with some kind of note or something. Clarence and I took the long way to the office, so Rayford must have taken the short, more obvious way but since he was new to the school he had to have been escorted. I didn't know exactly how Rayford got to class, but to be perfectly honest I didn't care. I was just happy he was there. As I took my seat we looked at each other and smiled.

The first day of school eventually came to an end and after the bell rang releasing us, I walked home with Rayford and Clarence. Excited with the idea of being able to see the progress that Rayford had made on the fort, I told Clarence about it.

"Clarence, Rayford is building a fort in the woods, so we're going to go and see it now." Hearing my words, Rayford shook his head.

"Nope, there's no fort."

Disappointed I asked, "What happened?"

"I just changed my mind. My uncle told me one time, he said, 'Just because you start something that doesn't mean you have to finish it.'" Rayford continued, "After you left I lost interest in the fort. I don't know why. I just did, so I left it." There wasn't anything more for me to say about the fort so I dropped the subject and the three of us ended up talking about whatever came to our minds. There was something very special about our little group and I wasn't the only one who felt it. Clarence said that the three of us were ordained to be friends. I didn't know what ordained meant at the time. I did, however, know that it was something good.

Seemingly, in relation to Clarence's proclamation Rayford, in his smooth manner of speaking said, "Tight to the end."

As if scripted, Clarence replied in response, "Tight to the end." A smile quickly came over Rayford's face, but as quickly as it appeared it disappeared as Rayford stared at me with an expression of unmet expectation.

"Well?" he impatiently asked me.

I replied, "Well—what?"

"You're supposed to say tight to the end to show you're in agreement."

"Oh—well I didn't know." Rayford looked at Clarence then back at me.

"Why didn't you just follow Clarence's lead?" My silence must have been enough for Rayford to cease expressing his disappointment. For several steps there was no talking between us. Since I felt that I was the cause of the silence, I felt that it was my job to at least try to remedy the situation.

I broke the silence by saying, "Tight to the end." Rayford and Clarence tried not to laugh but their failed attempts resulted in just the opposite. Seeing and hearing them laugh let me know that my attempt was a success. It was a good afternoon.

# CHAPTER 4

# *Dump Rats*

The first week of third grade finally came to an end. Rayford, Clarence and I, as had become our habit, walked home from school together. With no lack of things to talk about we kept a constant chatter until arriving at the head of my street. I lived the closest to our elementary school. I said goodbye to my new friends and proceeded down my street to my house. When I arrived home, I went straight to my room and fell backwards across my bed. While lying there, I stared at the various lines in the textured ceiling of my room until my mother came in.

She asked, "Is everything alright George?" As I began to answer a yawn overtook my words.

A garbled, "Yes, I'm just tired mom," came out. My mother shook her head with an entertained expression on her face. I knew that the amused expression meant that she was in a good mood, understood and accepted my answer. She told me that she had a cake baking in the oven. I sat up. My eyes opened wide. "What kind?" I asked.

"Oh I don't know," She said. "I guess you'll have to wait until after dinner to find out."

With a laugh in my voice I replied, "Oh mom."

She left my room repeating my words as she walked down the hall, "Oh mom, oh mom." I heard her laugh afterwards. It made me feel good. I flung myself backwards once again onto my bed to pick up where I had left off staring at my ceiling.

Somewhere between staring at my ceiling and daydreaming, I heard the doorbell ring. I sprang to my feet and peaked through the window blinds to see who was there. My room overlooked the front of the house. To my surprise, it was my Aunt Clare. I knew it was Aunt Claire because her car was parked in front of the house. I ran downstairs to let her inside. I always enjoyed my Aunt Clare's visits. She was fun and bubbly, and many times she shared stories about how my mother, Uncle Jesse and she grew up. Not long after sitting at the kitchen table talking mostly to my mother, Aunt Clare got the look in her eyes that always meant something good was going to happen.

"Who wants to hear a story?" she asked.

Smiling from ear to ear, my sister and I replied, "We do Aunt Clare." Returning our smiles she began.

"Ok! Well, you know we grew up at the foot of Rug Rat Alley, right?"

In unison and laughing my sister and I replied, "No Aunt Clare. You, mommy and Uncle Jesse grew up on Coleman Avenue."

Eyes twinkling, Aunt Clare continued, "Oh that's right Coleman Avenue." Aunt Clare turned to my mother and with a smile-laced seriousness said, "I guess it only seemed like Rug Rat Alley—huh Birdie?" Birdie is what Aunt Clare, Uncle Jessie and my grandmother called my mother. My mother's real name is Francis. They called her Birdie because they say she ate like a bird when they were kids.

In response to the question, my mother's face took on a light-hearted, relief stricken expression as she replied, "Oh don't remind me."

Turning her attention back to us, Aunt Clare continued, "Living on Coleman Avenue wasn't easy. We didn't have much, but I will tell you that we never went to sleep hungry. Daddy and Momma made sure of that."

"You mean grandpa and grandma?"

"That's right. Those are the exact daddy and momma I mean. Those were rough times back then—especially for Black people and even more for the Black kids, including your mother, Uncle Jesse and me, in our neighborhood."

Not understanding why it was particularly worse for that neighborhood, I asked, "Why?"

Aunt Clare simply said, "Because it was a Black neighborhood and very poor. I think the only reason grandpa was even able to afford our house is because it was near the city dump: being located near the dump made the prices of the houses in our neighborhood a little easier to afford. Can you believe that? The neighborhood we grew up in was in the same neighborhood as the city dump. Some of the kids at school who lived in different neighborhoods called your mother, me and Uncle Jesse Dump Rats. We hated that and we promised each other that we would live as far from a dump as we possibly could when we grew up."

"I'm never going to be poor Aunt Clare—never."

"Well George, if you keep making good grades, do what the teachers tell you to do and get a good job, you won't have to worry about that, now will you?"

With a determination and focus of which I'm sure Aunt Clare was not aware I replied, "No mam. I'm going to have a nice, beautiful house in a nice, beautiful neighborhood and be the happiest man in the world."

Beginning to think beyond what Aunt Clare had just shared, a puzzled look grew on my sister Michelle's face as well as mine.

We asked, "What dump? Grandpa and grandma still live on Coleman Avenue. Where's the dump?"

"Oh the city stopped dumping there years ago and covered it over with grass. You know the big hill not too far from grandpa and grandma's house?"

"Yes," we answered.

"That was the dump." Satisfied that everything lined up, my sister and I were content.

# CHAPTER 5

# *A Tight Fit*

September came and went without much excitement, as did the beginning and middle of October. Finally the end of October arrived, and Halloween day was upon us. The festivities started in school. We made cutouts of ghosts, and silhouettes of witches and black cats. Mrs. Cunningham had even brought in a record of Halloween stories and music to accompany our Halloween art activities. I may not have liked Mrs. Cunningham much at first, but as the days went on since the first day of school, I along with the other kids started to like her more and more. I think it was because she became more relaxed. We were her first teaching assignment, so I think she just needed time. By the end of September, I had even developed a little crush on her. She was by far the prettiest and youngest teacher I had ever had.

Fifteen minutes before the end of school Mrs. Cunningham handed out orange UNICEF boxes. They were flat and needed to be opened up and made into sturdy rectangular boxes. We were given UNICEF boxes in school ever since I can remember and although I didn't care much for raising money for starving kids, I loved putting the boxes together. I felt proud after folding the last cardboard flap into place and beholding my work.

Shortly after finishing the boxes, Mrs. Cunningham reminded us to incorporate our UNICEF fundraising into our night of trick or treating.

"Class, don't just say trick or treat when you go out tonight. Say trick or treat for UNICEF and hold your boxes out. There are children less fortunate then you who are in need of money so that they can eat and live a little better. Now, on three, let me hear what you're going to say tonight—one, two three."

"Trick or treat for UNICEF!" We must have done a good job because a huge smile grew on Mrs. Cunningham's face. Seconds after our shouted recitation the bell, ending school, rang and out of the class we ran.

Behind us we heard, "Slow down, no running, no running," in an ever increasingly fading voice. Full stride, Rayford, Clarence and I ran home eagerly anticipating a good evening of candy collecting.

Around 6pm that evening my father arrived home. My mother had dinner ready and had begun placing the plates and putting the food on the kitchen table as my father hung his coat and hat in the closet. After visiting the bathroom to wash his hands, he came to the kitchen and took his seat at the head of the table. We had a dining room, but the furniture was too nice to chance that my sister, brother or I would make a mess on it. My mother only allowed us to eat there for Thanksgiving, Christmas and Easter. After saying grace over the food, my father's opening words were about the temperature outside. He informed us that the temperature was forecasted to drop later that night. I had a funny feeling about this news.

After eating, I asked my mother if it were time to go trick or treating. Looking at the clock she responded, with not a great amount of enthusiasm.

"Ok, let's hurry up. I've got things to do." Unaffected by her lack of enthusiasm, I rushed upstairs to get my costume. Returning downstairs fully clad in my costume, I was met with a most confused look on my mother's face.

"Didn't you hear your father?" My face dropped. I knew exactly what that meant.

"Yes," I responded.

"Then take that costume off and get your winter coat on." Almost sullen I obeyed. Once I had on my winter coat, my very warm and thick, brown, corduroy winter coat, might I add, my mother proceeded to very gingerly put my Halloween costume over my coat. To this day I have no idea how she managed that feat without ripping the costume. There I stood looking as if the costume had been painted on by some expert artist trying to render the realism of stretch marks on delicate Halloween costume fabric. My sister was no doubt in the same boat, but I was oblivious to any emotional trauma she might have been experiencing. My focus was wholly on me. With not a shred of desire to have been the Hulk dressed as a cowboy, there I was, with the exception of being brown, this horrid hulk-like mistake of Halloween. More than amply prepared for anything this October's nightly gusts could summon, my mother, sister and I left our house and joined the fray of those out trick or treating.

It was no surprise to me, there weren't any other kids as warmly dressed as my sister and I. My mother believed in being prepared for the worst and she wasn't known for coming up short. She believed life was unpredictable enough without providing unpredictability. Rayford and Clarence lived a few blocks away. Fortunately, I didn't have to worry about running into them and having them tease me about my tight fitting costume. Very cautious about any evil that might be lurking about, my mother restricted trick or treating to our block and not one house beyond the limits of our block. Anything beyond that would have been in my mother's fear zone, and that would have been an act of tempting fate. Fortunately for my sister and me, we lived on a long street with plenty of houses.

Our street was really popular for trick or treating. As we walked I saw kids and their mothers scattered all about obliging porch light invitations to ring the doorbell and receive gifts of candy and coins. It was great walking around in costumes getting free candy and money, but what made it really special was being out at night and being able to be loud with my mother's permission. Breaking the night air with bellows of, "trick or treat for UNICEF!" with other kids was such an enjoyment for me.

When our night of trick or treating was over and we returned home, my mother reminded us of the Halloween candy rules of engagement:

1. *Unwrap the candy intended for consumption*
2. *Hold the wrapper to the light*
3. *Inspect the wrapper for holes and cuts*
4. *If wrapper is hole and cut free, the candy can be eaten providing it is within the allowable three-candy, after dinner limit*

Halloween had gotten pretty dangerous at that time. There were reports of people injecting candy with dangerous substances and placing razor blades in apples. There was no inspection of apples or any other fruit that might have been collected during trick or treating in my house. All such items were immediately tossed in the trash can. With the dangers of Halloween escalating, that may have very well been our last trick or treating as children, for I have no memories of any occurring after that Hulk of a Halloween.

# CHAPTER 6

# *A Need to Please*

Thanksgiving, Christmas and Easter came and went. Where my third grade year was going, I had no idea and before I knew it, it was over. The last day of school was on a Tuesday. To celebrate the first day of summer my mother and Clarence's mother took Clarence, my sister and me to the city zoo early the next morning. I remember the day being very special. To not be in school in the middle of the week and going to the zoo was really nice.

As soon as we got through the gates I yelled out, "We have to see the camels first." I quickly sought after a zoo directory. Shortly afterwards, I located the camels and was off leading the way to Camel Village.

Behind me I could hear murmurings of, "What's so special about the camels?" and "Why is he so eager to see them?" While ignoring their inquiries I lead the four, uninformed stragglers.

After determining the right time had come, I turned and informed them saying, "Visiting the camels will be our way of celebrating hump day."

Amidst a flurry of smiles, rolling eyes, playful attempts to discontinue our current direction and choruses of, "You gotta be kidding George," I widened my smile and employed a Camel Village bound strut the likes of which George Jefferson, of the *Jefferson's* television sitcom, would have been proud.

We made it to Camel Village, saw the camels then made our way to the elephants, antelopes, birds and monkeys. Our progression through the exhibits was by no means adequate to my liking. My mother was the type who loved learning, and however many information plaques were provided per exhibit, that's how many she read. She even made me listen and encouraged me to read along. I guess it was a good thing, but school had just let out and all I wanted to do was walk around, seeing and not reading about the animals. Because Clarence and my sister had no interest in indulging my mother's desire for reading the placards, and because they weren't people pleasers like I was, they chose their own items of interest on which to focus. On one occasion the item of interest was a fly that had been accidentally wounded and then eaten by an infant child. Admittedly I was equally interested in the spectacle but due to some deep seeded allegiance to obey and fulfill my mother's expectations, I denied myself the whimsical pleasure.

Clarence's mother never struck me as an information junkie, but she somehow managed to add enough to my mother's comments to keep things flowing nicely between the two of them. My focus was on pleasing my mother and to resist the distractions that were entertaining my sister and Clarence.

My mother's thirst for knowledge was sometimes hard to understand and when she went on for hours about some biological phenomenon, social dilemma, or political situation, it was equally as difficult to listen, especially when we were supposed to be in a fun, school-free environment. The whole reading, learning thing was boring at best. However, when it didn't look or sound like a class, boring she really wasn't. Her personality was warm and loving. She was one of the most effervescent souls anyone could ever meet. The case of Clarence and my sister not paying attention to her, I believe was my burden and not hers. I don't think she thought twice about it. I was the one with the feeling of obligation. My mother was in her zone and carefree.

After walking around for a while, Clarence got thirsty.

"Mom, I'm thirsty. Can I have a soda?"

Clarence's mother turned to him and replied, "You know, I'm kinda thirsty myself."

Seeing his opening Clarence added, "How about a hamburger too?"

Hearing this, my mother immediately spoke up, "Oh I've got some ham and cheese sandwiches and some drinks in the car." My eyes lit up.

"Yes," I said. I was hungry too but I knew better than to ask my mother to buy the overpriced food at the zoo. She would always say, "They should be ashamed of themselves charging those prices. That's highway robbery." I never really understood the significance of the highway. Nevertheless, I assure you I understood all too well the meaning and lesson behind the adage.

We made our way back to the entrance/exit gate of the zoo and there we got the backs of our hands stamped to allow our re-entry into the zoo once our lunch break was over.

As we walked to the car I heard my mother behind me again saying, "They should be ashamed of themselves charging those prices. That's highway robbery." I don't believe she was even speaking to anyone in particular. I think she was just expressing herself. My sister and I looked at each other and smiled. I picked up my pace. I was getting hungrier by the minute and could just about smell the ham and cheese sandwiches that were waiting for us in the car. What my mother had packed for us to drink was a mystery, but I knew I'd enjoy it. As it turned out, it ended up being iced tea. Nobody's iced tea was better than my mother's.

After lunch we returned to the zoo and, having only a few more animals and exhibits we wanted to see, my mother read every word on every plaque about them. Satisfied that she had adequately self-educated herself, we left. It was a wonderful day and a wonderful start to a good summer vacation. My mother and I went on several day trips that summer and subsequent summers following my third grade year. Never did my desire for my mother's approval wane. I simply wanted to do the right thing to make her proud of me.

# CHAPTER 7

# Lemons and Lemonade

I t was my seventh grade year, early autumn, when my grandparents' house caught on fire. It was horrible as all house fires are, but it was even worse because it was my grandparents' house. Immediately following the fire, unable to live in the house, they took up temporary residence with their two daughters. My grandmother came with us and my grandfather went with Aunt Clare and her family. My grandparents, unwilling to accept the batch of lemons that life had thrown them, didn't sit around pouting about their ill fate, though. Each focused on taking the beating that life had given them and became stronger for it. My grandparents put an old saying, "If life throws you lemons, make lemonade," into action. Over the course of several months, however, their ideas and plans of turning their lemons into lemonade took divergent paths.

My grandfather was a man who took pride in the strength and ability of his hands. He scrimped and saved for a long time to afford the house on Coleman Street and saw no reason to relinquish it to the powers of a fire. For many months he worked hard to rebuild his house. I would imagine my grandmother shared my grandfather's desire and will to rebuild to return to their house, but seeing the permanent ravages of fire upon their home a different viewpoint came to my grandmother. After seeing what my grandfather had accomplished or probably was unable to accomplish over the course of several months, regarding the refurbishing of their house, my grandmother's desires to return departed.

Fixed on his initial viewpoint, my grandfather refused to see, or was incapable of seeing things from my grandmother's viewpoint. He got the house, in his estimation, to a decent level to return and did in fact return with the assumption that his unhappy wife would follow. She did not. She didn't feel the house was up to standards for her to return. She wanted more than a shell of a house. Both were bent on taking the sour lemons and making something sweet. Unable to agree on a single path, however, they proceeded in different directions. My grandfather ended up back in his house, while my grandmother chose to move into an apartment. They were both alone.

The divergent paths chosen by my grandparents weren't without an effect on the family dynamics. Former drives to Coleman Street to visit my grandparents somehow turned into drives to only see my grandmother at her apartment. There were never any drives to Coleman Street to see my grandfather. It was like my grandfather had become non-existent. The adults of the family didn't talk much about these matters.

Consequently, the virtual loss of my grandfather resulted in me only knowing about where and how my grandmother lived. My grandmother's apartment was on the first floor of a four story apartment building. Each floor, with the exception of the first, had six apartments. The first floor had eight. My grandmother's apartment was the first one on the left upon entering the building. The hallway to her apartment was always dimly lit.

It had a distinct odor that I can smell to this day. The odor was neither bad nor good. It was just distinct. The door leading into her apartment opened to a landing from which ten steps descended to the floor of her apartment. It was a small, one bedroom apartment. It was so small, that she didn't have space for a normal, house-sized washer and dryer. As a space saving alternative, she purchased a washer and dryer unit where the dryer sat on top of the washer.

Salvaged from the fire, some of my grandmother's furniture was moved from Coleman Avenue to the apartment. Possibly one of her most beloved furniture pieces was her buffet. On the top of the buffet, she proudly displayed her holiday crystal. The sofa, opposite the buffet, was on the north wall of the living room. Her dining room table set was larger than what the apartment could comfortably accommodate. Determined to keep it, though, she placed it length-wise along the west wall of her apartment. It was an eight chair dining room table set. To allow room to access the kitchen, the three dining room chairs along the west wall were rendered useless as they were pinned between the table and the west wall. Separating the dining room from the kitchen was a half wall which extended eastward from the west wall. Its width was a foot or so shy of the depth of the dining room table. My grandmother's bedroom seemed quite small. It might have been about a twelve by twelve room. The size of the room didn't stop her from filling it with items she felt her bedroom should have though. She had a queen size bed with a large hardwood head and foot board, along with a matching dresser and end table. The space between the side of her bed and her dresser would not allow two adults to stand side by side.

One item I always enjoyed looking at was a picture of an old, but striking wooden church. If it hung on any wall at Coleman Street I never noticed it. When I noticed it in the apartment, I asked about it and was given the story behind it. The church in the picture was the family church. Family was always a big thing for me. For years, prior to my birth, the family worshipped, mourned deaths and celebrated life in that old church.

As years passed, as the story was told to me, the old wooden church was torn down to make room for a new, more accommodating and progressive looking church. After the church was torn down, the family splintered to different churches in the area. The family church was no more. The impact of the story on me as a child was strong. I internalized a loss. After learning the history of the church, whenever I was in my grandmother's bedroom, I stared at it. It always touched me emotionally.

With the trauma of the fire and my grandmother's hard decision fading more and more, her new living quarters were becoming a home—her home. My grandmother, indeed, took the lemons of the fire and made an apartment into what I guess amounted to lemonade.

What transpired with my grandfather, I don't know. All I know is that he put his best foot forward to sweeten the lemons that were left from the fire. Whether he made lemonade or not, I do not know. I do know, however, that from the fire, I lost my grandfather and that is quite a sour reality. One person's lemonade may not be to the liking of another person, but to each is given an empty lemonade pitcher. The choice to make lemonade or not is up to each person just as the choice of how sweet or tart to make the batch.

# CHAPTER 8

# The Sad Truth

With the unsettling impact of the fire behind us, I started my eighth grade school year with my grandmother getting more and more accustomed to living on her own and our family, as a whole, happy and pretty much back to business as usual. I was happy. Placing a particular smile on my face was the news I received on Thursday of the first week of school. I found out that I made the starting lineup of my middle school's football team. I was a proud Booker T. Washington Eagle. Being a new Eagle I wanted to live up to the expectations the coach had of our team and particularly those of us who were selected to start. Coach T, as we called him, worked us hard. He said he was preparing us for a banner football season as well as key positions on our high school team—The Oak Bridge High School Bears.

During the second week of practice, after one of our grueling workouts, I had a hankering for a soda. There was a corner store, two blocks from school opposite a street called Preston Road. It wasn't on my normal route home, but it wasn't grossly out of the way. I decided to head to the store for a quick purchase of a soda. The store had the cheapest price in town for canned sodas. As I walked, a girl named Natalie Goldberg popped in my mind. She lived on Preston Road. I didn't know her from school. She didn't attend Booker T or even my elementary school. We met through our mothers. Our mothers knew each other through my grandmother's relationship with Natalie's grandparents—Dr. and Mrs. Solomon Schwartz. My grandmother at one time cleaned house for the Schwartz. Somewhere along the way my mother met Natalie's mother and became friends.

In my early, elementary school years, my mother would visit Natalie's mother. She usually brought me along. It wasn't often, but it was enough for an elementary school-aged boy to begin his understanding that girls can make boys feel things that were simultaneously foreign and favorable.

I remember the first time I met Natalie. My mother paid Mrs. Goldberg a visit with me in tow. My mother and Natalie's mother talked and laughed until eventually Mrs. Goldberg realized that I was as bored as I could be. She asked me if I would like to go upstairs and play with her daughters. Not waiting for my reply, Mrs. Goldberg called to her daughters to come downstairs while simultaneously, but gently, pushing me on my back encouraging me to walk up the steps with instructions on how to get to the attic, where apparently the girls were playing. Meeting the two girls close to the top of the stairs, Mrs. Goldberg informed them that I was visiting, and instructed them to include me in their playing. They led me to the attic where they had been playing a board game. I was uncomfortable being in a new place with new faces, but Natalie and her sister were very nice and in a short time, I became a little less uncomfortable. Natalie and I were both about seven years old. I was captivated by her. I had never been affected by a girl the way I was affected by Natalie. Being next to her kept me uncomfortable, but it wasn't an uncomfortable feeling from which I wished to be separated. On the contrary, it was a feeling I most particularly enjoyed.

I wasn't familiar with the game the sisters were playing, but after Natalie took the time to explain the rules I understood the goal and how to play. It turned out to be an easy game to play. Although it was easy, the last thing I wanted to do was mess-up in front of Natalie. Who would believe a seven year old could feel this way?

Subsequent visits to Natalie's home were no different from the first—pleasurably uncomfortable. I was a shy kid and I was completely enamored by Natalie. As much as I enjoyed being around her, I hated how awkward I felt. I never said much around her. I remember always having the hope that she simply thought that I was shy and not unhappy to be around her.

As the elementary years rolled by the visits to the Goldberg's became fewer and fewer. By the beginning of my sixth grade year, if my mother visited, she did so without me. I don't know. The Christmas of my sixth grade year, I got a new bicycle. I missed seeing Natalie. I decided that once the weather warmed up I would ride my new bike by her house.

Beginning the following summer, I frequently rode up and down Preston Road with hopes of seeing her. Most of the trips were without success, but a couple of times I got lucky. One lucky time was when I saw her get into her parents' car and another time I faintly saw her walk by the front, screen door of her house.

By mid-summer I had an accident. I was trying to be like Evel Knievel and ended up destroying my bike. That ended any more chance glimpses of Natalie. I didn't see her until the arbitrary day, after football practice, when Natalie popped in my mind on my way to the corner store across from Preston Road.

After leaving the corner store I opened my soda can while staring across Delmar Street to Preston Road. I drew a deep breath and proceeded to cross Delmar heading straight for Preston. It had been a while since I had been on Preston Road, but as I walked down Preston and got closer to Natalie's house, the feelings I used to have for her came rushing back.

At this point, Natalie's family was the only white family on Preston Road, when at one time it was all white. As Black families moved in, the white families moved away. I was aware of the change on the street, but it didn't have much meaning or impact on me. As I was passing Natalie's house, I saw a figure on the porch. It was Natalie. I recognized her right away; she was still beautiful. She was reading a book. My heart began to beat fast and hard. I took another deep breath and swallowed as I tried to figure out what I should do next. In the past, when I was lucky to see her as I was riding my bike by her house, I never really had an opportunity to say anything. This time was different. I was on foot and she was there, in plain view on the porch.

I decided that I should say hello or something, but just as I was about to open my mouth I asked myself, "Ok—what should I do after I say hi? If I stop to talk, what should I say and what should I do if she puts her head back into her book after rendering the polite hello in response to mine? Do I just keep walking?" Awkward, stiff and looking forward, with no variance, I walked by without saying a single word. I hated myself.

I didn't have the courage to go through this the next day, but I did try it again walking home after a few more football practices. For me, Natalie was in a league of her own. She wasn't simply another girl. She was on a different level: a level to which I simply couldn't raise myself. I simply didn't have the confidence. I eventually gave up on a chance conversation with her. I discontinued my Preston Road torture trips.

Sometime between Halloween and Thanksgiving of that year I was in the kitchen talking to my mother as she was preparing dinner. As we casually talked she mentioned that the Goldbergs had moved from Preston Road to the "ritzy," as my mother called it, part of town. I got a little sad, but I realized nothing had really changed. Natalie's new residence was figuratively just as far or near as her Preston Road residence had been to me.

# CHAPTER 9

# A Moment of Intersection

"Grey, I said it once and I'll say it again, alot of guys would love to have your life. You're a successful, middle class family man. You attended a prestigious Black College and graduated from one of the top high schools in the nation: the preppy, prestigious Davis Prep. That school is the only private high school in the City of Oak Bridge; that says something. I remember you transferred there in your sophomore year and according to what Clarence told me, you had it going on up at The Prep. Clarence said he visited your school on some type of exchange program between Oak Bridge and Davis Prep. Some of the Oak Bridge High kids went to Davis Prep and vice versa. I also heard that all those rich girls knew you. Hey—by the way, what happened to Natalie?" I began to smile as I listened to Rayford recall the student exchange day between Davis Preparatory and my first high school—Oak Bridge High School.

The day I learned that Oak Bridge High School exchange students were visiting Davis Prep was the time I was in the student government room. The exchange program involved the Student Government Associations of both schools. Before that day, though, I had never stepped foot in any student government room. I never even thought much about student government beyond voting for the person who was first on the ballot. Student government was never of any interest to me. It just didn't hold my attention. Besides, depending on the season, I was either training for or playing football, working on the yearbook or involved in track and field. The way I ended up in the student government room was beyond anything I could have imagined or anticipated. Ending up there occurred one winter, school morning in my junior year. Being there that day, however, would not have happened if it were not for what occurred on my first day at Davis Prep.

In my new homeroom, as a new Davis Prep sophomore, I sat awaiting the start of my new academic life when in walked this beauty of a girl. It was Natalie Goldberg. Seeing Natalie standing in the doorway was surreal. My mind raced as all of my old thoughts of her were suddenly released in a rush of controlled excitement. Our eyes met. I think she recognized me immediately. Her smile made me think so. She sat in the vacant desk in front of mine. She faced me with her elbows on my desk. I managed to stay cool and to not melt from the heat of her presence.

She was as confident and friendly as I remember she had been. Her eyes were fixed on mine as she asked how I had been and how I ended up at Davis Prep. I was still intimidated by her beauty and still didn't want to mess-up by doing or saying anything out of place, but fortunately I had done some maturing over the years. I could now actually talk to her without being a barely-communicative bundle of nerves. I answered her questions and then asked how she had been. The affect this girl still had on me was mind boggling, but I wouldn't have traded those feelings for any others in the world.

In the days and weeks that followed, Natalie and I did a great deal of catching up—most of which was done in homeroom. Usually after homeroom we wouldn't see each other but for momentary glances and smiles as we passed in the hallways in route to our classes.

One chilly February morning, in homeroom in my junior year at Davis Prep, Natalie and I were busy talking as had become our habit. With ten or so minutes left of homeroom, Natalie asked me if I wanted to leave a few minutes earlier.

Not taking her particularly seriously, I answered, "sure." Natalie rose from her chair and walked over to our homeroom teacher, Mrs. Neil. After a brief few moments talking to Mrs. Neil, Natalie turned and beckoned me to join her in exiting the classroom. The first thing out of my mouth as our homeroom door closed behind us was, "What did you tell Mrs. Neil? Why did she let us leave early?"

Natalie smiled and answered, "Because I have to go to the student government room and I wanted some company." Before she even got the word company fully out of her mouth she gave my side a good pinch then giggled and ran off. Knowing girls as I had come to know them, I knew that the pinch, as painful as it was, was a flirtatious statement of prerogative. When a girl likes a guy she will, from time to time, do or say things to him that would be found socially unacceptable had those things been imposed upon her by the guy. It's one of the great gender double standards. Because I had also come to know that the flirtatious acts of girls should never be immediately concluded to mean that the girl is interested in a boyfriend girlfriend relationship, I simply accepted the flesh damaging pinch as a friendly, flirtatious gesture and obliged it by running after her, while at the same time speaking empty threats that she clearly enjoyed.

We came to an abrupt halt when we heard, "No running in the hallway!" It came bellowing out from behind us. It was Principal McKinney. He asked where we were going and why we were in such a hurry.

Natalie explained, "We are rushing to avoid being late for the Exchange Program Meet-and-Greet."

"Exchange Program Meet-and-Greet?" I questioned in my mind.

"I'll accept that as an explanation for you running Miss Goldberg, but I don't see the connection to Mr. Grey. Unless I'm mistaken Mr. Grey is not a student government member."

Very nervously, I began to search for words. "Well, sir, I . . ."

Natalie cut me off, "Principal McKinney, I just thought it would be a nice surprise. Mr. Grey could also greet the visiting student government exchange students, if you know what I mean. I felt it would mean alot to him and to them as well." My nervousness changed to confusion. Natalie continued, "To be perfectly honest Mr. McKinney, Mr. Grey doesn't even know what's going on. I just dragged him along." I was ignorant of the exchange program, but even more to the point, I was ignorant of my relation to the special circumstances surrounding this particular exchange program: circumstances I later came to realized that were the reason Principal McKinney was so agreeable to the surprise Natalie had cooked up.

Principal McKinney let us go with one simple instruction, "Don't run anybody over in your haste." It was at that moment Natalie went from being the most beautiful girl in the world to being the most magical girl in the world as well. I had no other way of explaining how Principal McKinney permitted us to resume running in the hall with the gift of a friendly caution to not run anyone over.

Natalie and I parted company with Principal McKinney on the fondest of terms.

Distancing ourselves from him, I looked over at Natalie as we hurriedly made our way to the student government room and asked, "What just happened?" Natalie smiled and speeded up her pace.

Positioned now slightly ahead of me she looked back and with a playful sarcasm remarked, "Surely those athletic legs can move faster than that!"

Laughing and feeling great, we arrived at the student government room. There was a great deal of activity and somewhere in the midst of it all, I heard that some students from Oak Bridge High School had arrived and they were about to be dismissed from the meet-and-greet in the auditorium.

Upon hearing this I smiled, looked at Natalie and simply said, "Ahh, nice work Miss Goldberg, nice work."

Natalie was one of the escorts. Realizing she wouldn't be in time for the meet-and-greet Natalie requested the name of the Oak Bridge student she would be escorting. With the name secured she hurried to the door to be on her way to the auditorium. Still smiling and preoccupied with my newly acquired knowledge of what Natalie's intentions were and the confident manner in which she dealt with Principal McKinney, I wasn't aware that she was holding the door waiting for me.

"Hey you over there—day dreamer, I'm not done with you yet. Bring your smiling self along." My head and attention turned so fast toward Natalie that I became a little light headed. I think that's what caused me to stumble as I walked toward her. My stumbling resulted in her shaking her head with a warm, affection-assuring smile. At her side once again, we made a dash to the auditorium. "Watch your step," she cautioned with a glorious smile across her face.

"Haha," I pleasantly replied with full and glorious sarcasm.

As we neared the auditorium I could see a small group of Davis Prep and Oak Bridge students quietly clamoring just outside the auditorium doors. Since I used to attend Oak Bridge I saw several familiar faces. Joining the small group, I hugged the Oak Bridge High girls I knew and coolly greeted the Oak Bridge guys with strong, multi-step handshakes suggestive of a brotherhood worthy of mention, notice and desire. The

Davis Prep escorts looked on, interested and possibly even captivated. If I can put it in terms of cake, the Davis Prep student body was like marble cake with very little marble, while the Oak Bridge student body was of the German chocolate cake persuasion—like I am. German chocolate cake is obviously chocolate but what really makes it interesting cake is the icing. The icing really gives it its flavor or as some might say,—its flava. I believe that the greeting between my Oak Bridge acquaintances and me was akin to a small sampling of German chocolate cake icing for the Davis Prep escorts.

As I was about to make a dash for my first period class, I couldn't help but notice the Oak Bridge guys looking at Natalie. Natalie, as well as the rest of the escorts, was not of the German chocolate persuasion, but regardless of her cake persuasion she drew the attention of anyone who appreciated a well baked cake. She wasn't my girlfriend but I was plenty jealous. I think it's safe to say that the Oak Bridge exchange program girls were jealous as well, albeit for a different reason from mine.

Just as I took a step to make my break for class, the auditorium door opened and out came Clarence. I stopped dead in my tracks.

"Clarence!"

Clarence's attention turned to me and as we each walked to greet the other, in full grin he blurted out, "Man, I was hoping I was gonna see you today!" Just as we ended our greeting the first period late bell rang. Turning to run to class I told Clarence I'd see him later. I caught Natalie's eye. We both smiled.

I didn't see Clarence until later that day, but in all my classes leading up to seeing him, it seemed as though all the girls wanted to know if I knew the boys who were visiting from Oak Bridge. Once I confirmed that I knew them, they wanted to know how I knew them and how well I knew them. They didn't know that I had transferred from Oak Bridge High.

More than a few of the girls specifically asked if I knew the Oak Bridge boy who had the big Michael Jackson afro; the one in question was Clarence. They told me he was the coolest. I guess some guys might have become jealous from being questioned by girls about other guys, but I got my fair share of German chocolate cake attention at school and that day, I felt like a superstar from all the extra attention I received from simply knowing the male students from Oak Bridge High.

At the end of the day Clarence and I got a chance to talk a short while before he and the other Oak Bridge students boarded their buses to leave Davis Prep.

When it was time for them to head for their bus, Clarence and I shook our style of hand shake then he said, "Tight to the end bro."

I smiled and replied, "Tight to the end," in response.


Finally snapping to what Rayford had just said I asked, "And what do you know about Natalie?"

With a big grin on his face, Rayford replied, "Oh Clarence told a brotha about a certain snow white delight up in Vanilla Village that day!" Turning to Clarence with a surprised look on my face I asked Rayford what exactly Clarence had told him about Natalie. Clarence stood up from the porch chair and leaned on the wooden banister.

"Grey, after you left to get to your class, Natalie, who at the time was a mere nameless beauty to me, raised her voice, 'Excuse me, is Clarence Davenport here?' I pinched myself to make sure I wasn't dreaming then I raised my hand telling her here I am. She told me that she was my escort for the day then away we went. But let me tell you. Grey—after telling me her name, the only thing that girl talked about was George this and George that and in every class I heard the same thing from the other girls. I should have been mad, but how could I be mad with all those girls around me, especially Natalie."

Hardly believing what I had just heard, I spoke up, "I don't believe you Clarence. If memory serves me correctly, all I heard that day was every girl asking me who you were. All I heard was Michael Jackson afro this and Michael Jackson afro that." The three of us, upon hearing all of this for the first time, burst into laughter until our sides ached.

After calming down Rayford asked me, "So what happened between you and Natalie?"

Dumfounded I answered, "The big donut. Nothing, nothing at all happened between Natalie and me. I was too scared to really make a move. I thought she liked me, but I wasn't sure. I was just too scared."

It was true that I had gained confidence since my earlier dealings with Natalie, but I was still intimidated by her, and being older I had become cautious of the Black White issue. I didn't want to be rejected. It was better for me to keep hidden, the special feelings I had for her. I thought she liked me, but I just didn't believe in myself enough. I was just too scared.

Looking back, the day of the exchange program with Oak Bridge High School was a day very different from any other day I experienced at Davis Prep. Since transferring to Davis Prep, there were two worlds in which I lived. The one I left in the morning—the world where I was reared—the German chocolate cake world and the one I left in the afternoon—the marble cake world with its scarcity (numbering six out of a couple hundred) of marble strands. In the Davis Prep world, money, cars, boats and big houses were in abundance; not so in the Oak Bridge world. I believe the six strands of marble were probably the only marble that many, if not most, of the Davis Prep students knew personally—with the exception of their housekeepers. The reason the exchange day was so different from any other day at Davis Prep was because for one brief moment, the two worlds I had come to know as my life, intersected and it felt really good.

Living in two worlds, I ended up juggling the two. It wasn't difficult; it was just part of my life. When I first transferred to Davis Prep my weekends were unchanged. I spent them all in the Oak Bridge world, but by the spring of my sophomore year things began to change. I started getting invitations to parties and to simply hang out with my new, Davis Prep world friends. The times I hung out with them I was the sole strand of marble in the marble cake. At first it was a little strange. I was self-conscious, but after a while I simply regarded them as friends. Clarence and Rayford were the only Oak Bridge people I truly considered friends and hence they were the ones I hung out with when I wasn't with my school friends. Although I spent more time with my school friends than with either Rayford or Clarence, my bond with Clarence and Rayford was deeper than my bond with my school friends. I guess having school friends afforded me with more opportunities to make out-of-school plans or maybe there was an interest and intrigue with the Davis Prep world. I can't say I honestly know, but I also can't honestly say that I think it mattered.

# CHAPTER 10

# Good Times

Still stuck on why I didn't do anything towards a possible relationship with Natalie, Rayford, with a teasing sort of confused facial expression, asked, "You were scared?" I wasn't about to dignify his question. I had already humbled myself by confessing that I was too afraid to put my German chocolate neck out on the line.

I simply responded, "Hey—my queen's in the house. Where's yours?"

Rayford was divorced; he simply nodded his head with a smirk of admitted surrender followed with, "Ok—you scored. You got me."

Clarence added a timely, "Ouch," and within seconds the three of us broke out into laughter once again.

The summer following my sophomore year was more of the same of how my life had changed since transferring to Davis Prep; I lived in two worlds. With my Davis Prep friends, I drove around upper class neighborhoods in expensive cars, went to upper class parties, frequented the rock section of record stores and soaked in, as much as a slice of German chocolate cake cares to soak in, the tanning rays of the sun while yachting on river ways where in years prior to Davis Prep, I had only traveled over by bridge.

With Rayford and Clarence I played basketball, went to movies, sang in the church choir, rode bikes, girl-watched along the avenue and stuffed my face at our favorite place to eat—Luigi's Pizzeria. Luigi's was a part of Rayford's and Clarence's and my high school experience. One late summer day at Luigi's, we made a pact that we would celebrate our graduation from high school by eating at Luigi's the day after our graduations. It would signify the ending of an era.

One day during the same summer, Rayford and Clarence came by my parents' house to see if I was interested in playing basketball with them. I hadn't hung out with them for a few weeks so I was most definitely interested. We walked from my house to our favorite spot to play—the parking lot court of our former middle school. As we walked we dribbled and passed the ball around talking about whatever came to our minds. Once at the court we played hard. We rotated between playing one-on-one games and *Twenty One*. *Twenty One* allowed all three of us to play at the same time. We played until we were exhausted.

There was something in the chemistry between Rayford and me that erupted frequently. We competed for dominance and control in many areas of our lives. Unlike Clarence, who was a gentle spirit off the court, but who rose to the challenge of a competition only to return to his gentle disposition afterwards, Rayford and I seemed to maintain a competitive disposition with respect to each other. With or without a particular event of competition, Rayford and I seemed to always be poised to prove something to each other. Which of us was better was very important to us. Gratefully, our maintained disposition of engagement was never mean spirited. In fact our encounters for dominance made me a better competitor. So I just might owe my spot on the varsity football team to Rayford.

After managing to drum up enough energy to make it back to my parents' house, we discovered my parents were not home. We were a little disappointed because had my mother been home she would have undoubtedly had something for us to eat. We did, however, find enough to drink. Somewhat rejuvenated, we ended up out on the porch and once again Rayford and I were at it. Somehow we ended up entangled like two Sumo wrestlers trying to see who could displace whose footing first. In a split second after Rayford had managed to get me off balance I found my back crashing into the glass pane of the storm door. Immediately the horseplay stopped. We all stared at the broken pane and all three of us knew we were in trouble. We had two options. Do nothing and get what was coming to us by my parents or try to do something and at least get some credit for trying to be responsible. We chose option two.

We scrounged up a couple of dollars between the three of us, cleaned up the mess, took measurements and set out on foot to the local hardware store. We bought the replacement pane, walked back to my parents' house and proceeded to install the pane. Everything was going nicely. My parents were nowhere in sight and the door pane was almost perfectly set in place until we heard a little snap. We hadn't cleared a small piece of glass from the last corner of the frame and from the pressure of trying to fit the new pane into the last corner of the frame, an arching crack appeared in the corner of the pane. It was very small, but to us it stood out like a sore thumb.

After a brief, joy-deflating silence I spoke up, "I won't say anything if you two don't." Rayford and Clarence agreed. To our amazement it all worked out. My parents never said anything, but somehow, now being a parent myself, I have a sneaky suspicion they knew. They just chose not to say anything. Kids really don't know how much mercy is extended to them by their parents. Sometimes, though, mercy is far from what parents have in mind.

As our laugher subsided, Clarence's mind somehow wondered to my father. He asked me how my father was doing. My father had recently come down with an illness.

"He's doing ok. It looks like he's on the mend," I told him. With a retrospective gleam in his eyes, Clarence stared off into space.

Turning his attention back to me and wearing a smile he shared some feelings about my father and my father's brothers, "Grey, your dad and your uncles were wild. They were really nice guys, but boy sometimes they could be like merciless sharks. I remember one Christmas one of your girl cousins—I think it was Keisha—well she brought a boyfriend to your family's annual Christmas Eve get-together-sing-a-long. They ate him alive. They threw him around like he was some kind of play thing."

Fully relating to what Clarence was saying, Rayford nodded his head a couple of times and added his two cents, "Your dad and your uncles were like us." Clarence's head jerked towards Rayford.

"What do you mean like us? We never tore into people like they did."

Tickled, Rayford explained himself, "No, that's not what I mean. You know how we used to throw the baseball around? Those balls got no respect from us. If we weren't throwing a fast ball over a rock-scratched home plate, we were throwing all sorts of grounders and high balls—sometimes on dirt, sometimes on the grass but mostly on the street. We tore up alot of balls." Clearly still tickled Rayford continued, "Grey's father and his uncles were just like us but instead of a baseball they were throwing around some poor dude who didn't know enough to stay away from the girls in Grey's family." Rayford's clarification led to an amen from Clarence. "I'm just glad I was never their ball." I couldn't help but see Rayford's point. The men in my family could be rough characters. They meant no harm, but if the mood hit them to play a little catch you better hope they didn't have you selected as the ball.

# CHAPTER 11

# *Ending of Eras*

My senior year at Davis Prep finally came. It would have been the perfect year had it not been for a sadness that crept in unexpectedly in early November. I was sitting in my homeroom talking to some friends when I noticed that Natalie wasn't in her seat. For the past several weeks she hadn't been feeling too well. I guessed that maybe she had come down with a virus or something until I spotted her through the window of our homeroom door. I tried several times to catch her attention but was unable. She looked sad and distant. I kept staring at her and wondering why she was standing just outside the door and why Mrs. Hartford, our homeroom teacher, didn't tell her to come inside. There was no way Mrs. Hartford didn't notice Natalie standing there. With an expression of concerned confusion across my face I continued trying to get Natalie's attention until suddenly she looked at me with what appeared to be watery eyes. Seconds later, she waved to me and then walked away. I rose from my seat and began to walk towards the door.

Mrs. Hartford called out, "Mr. Grey, have a seat." I have never been in the habit or practice of ignoring my elders but that day I did. I paid no attention to Mrs. Hartford and continued to and out of the homeroom door. In the hallway I looked for Natalie. She was nowhere in sight. An uncomfortable feeling grew in the pit of my stomach. I walked back into my homeroom and took my seat without as much as even a gentle reprimand from Mrs. Hartford.

When the bell rang to end homeroom, I walked to Mrs. Hartford's desk. Embarrassed, I apologized to her for my rude behavior.

A certain look in her eyes led me to ask, "Mrs. Hartford, did you see Natalie outside the door a few minutes ago?" Mrs. Hartford knew that Natalie and I were good friends. She looked at me as she was deciding whether or not to answer.

Once she decided, she responded with calculated words, "Something has come up George. Natalie won't be with us anymore."

Respectfully I asked, "Something came up? What do you mean, Mrs. Hartford, something like what?"

Uncomfortable, Mrs. Hartford answered, "George if Natalie wanted you to know she would have told you. Now please get your books and get to your first period class. The late bell is about to ring."

Natalie and I were largely school friends. Beyond a chance meeting on some weekend, our times together were limited to school. We lived at opposite ends of the city and hung out in social circles that never intersected. Despite these limitations, though, we forged a formidable friendship. It was for reasons of our strong friendship that I simply couldn't understand why I was in the dark with respect to Natalie not being with us anymore. I was sad and confused, but mostly I was hurt.

Over the next several weeks, leading up to the last school day before Christmas break, hall chatter regarding Natalie's departure was the gossip de jour. I didn't hear the truth from Natalie so I refused to believe anything I heard. She was my good friend and I felt that I owed her that respect.

Over the Christmas break I looked up Natalie's parents' telephone number in my mother's address and phone book. I called the Saturday before Christmas.

Mrs. Goldberg answered, "Hello."

"Hello, Mrs. Goldberg, this is George Grey, Francis Grey's son."

A bit aloof Mrs. Goldberg answered, "Oh yes—hello George how may I help you?"

"Uh, I was wondering if I could talk to Natalie for a moment."

Still aloof, Mrs. Goldberg answered, "Natalie isn't home at the moment George."

Determined to get some answers I asked, "When would be a good time for me to call back?"

Pointedly, Mrs. Goldberg answered, "George, you know, I don't think that's going to be possible. Natalie is quite busy, but I'll tell her that you called. You have a lovely day now and tell your mother I said hello. Bye now." The next sound I heard was that of Mrs. Goldberg hanging up. I wanted to call her back just to hang up on her.

As if speaking to another person in the room, I asked aloud, "Did Mrs. Goldberg just hang up on me?" Within myself I debated the issues. After giving up, I went to the kitchen.

My mother was cooking dinner.

"Hey mom, you don't visit Mrs. Goldberg anymore do you?"

Without looking up from her work, my mother answered, "No, I haven't seen Shana in a long time." My mother's answer made some of my bad feelings disappear. I knew Mrs. Goldberg's first name was Shana but prior to that day, whenever my mother spoke to me with any reference to her, she always used Mrs. Goldberg. My mother's use of Mrs. Goldberg's first name made me feel like I was an adult or at least less like a child. I wore a smile on my face that I assume my mother found peculiar. "What are you smiling at George?" My smile grew.

"Uhh—nothing mom." With a distrustful expression on her face, my mother then asked about my interest in Mrs. Goldberg.

"So what's the sudden interest in Mrs. Goldberg?"

"I don't know mom. I go to school with her daughter. We're actually good friends and before the break she just left school for some mysterious reason."

"Well, you know it's probably just mysterious to you. I'm quite sure both Natalie and her mother know the reason."

"Yeah, well that's just it. I just called Mrs. Goldberg to ask if I could speak to Natalie and she basically hung up in my face."

"Oh—now come on George, that doesn't sound like Mrs. Goldberg to me. You mean to tell me that you called her on the phone, she answered the phone and after you introduced yourself and asked for Natalie, she just hung up?"

"Well, no but . . ."

" . . . but what? Tell me exactly what happened."

I sighed then continued, "I called the house and Mrs. Goldberg answered. Then I introduced myself and asked if I could speak to Natalie. Mrs. Goldberg told me that Natalie wasn't home. Then when I asked her when would be a good time for me to call back, she said Natalie was busy, told me to have a nice day and then hung up on me."

My mother thought deeply about what I had just shared.

Then she responded, "Well, that still doesn't sound like Shana but I'm sure she had her reasons. Who knows, after Christmas break, Natalie might be back at school and she'll be able to tell you all of what happened including her mother's coldness on the phone."

I thought about what my mother said and responded with a half believed, "Maybe." I kissed my mother on the cheek and went to my room. I stayed there until it was time for dinner.

Sitting in my room I considered calling a friend or two about Natalie but decided against it. After thinking about it I didn't see any benefit that could come out of calling any friends. I didn't want to hear any unsubstantiated speculations. I needed to hear what was going on from Natalie. It was clear, however, Natalie didn't want me to know. I decided to let it go and to more seriously consider my mother's words. Maybe, in fact, Natalie would be back in January and would fill in all of the missing pieces.

Following an otherwise uneventful but good Christmas break, I returned to school. There was no sign of Natalie, though. I wondered if she and her family had moved again but this time out of the city, state or even the country. Though I was sad that I hadn't seen her, I was happy that the hall talk concerning her departure was nowhere to be found.

As the days and weeks turned into months, thoughts of my absent friend significantly lessened and I became increasingly occupied with the anticipation of graduation and entering college. I found no pleasure, however, in the college application process. I would have preferred to have been simply assigned to a college to attend.

The second semester shot by and before I knew it, graduation day had arrived. It was convenient that Oak Bridge High and Davis Prep's commencement services were on different days. That fact made it possible for Clarence and Rayford to attend my graduation and for me to attend theirs.

The day after Oak Bridge's graduation, which followed Davis Prep's graduation, Rayford, Clarence and I kept our plan to go to Luigi's for our private graduation celebration. I drove us there. At the table we talked nonstop. We reminisced over the days long gone and not so long gone. Rayford talked about enlisting in the army and shared his dreams of being a military man. Clarence shared his heart's desire to be an instrument of God to lead people to Christ. I didn't have any significant plans or dreams for the future. For me, my future was merely the continuation of school. Once again I would proceed to the next academic campus to successfully navigate its academic ladder of matriculation. The first year of college, to me, was merely thirteenth grade: the next grade after twelfth grade.

As our pizzeria celebration neared its end, a bit of sadness fell upon us. In a few short weeks our trio would be broken up. Clarence and I would be attending the same college in Atlanta, but Rayford would be wherever Uncle Sam wanted him to be. We rose from our chairs and looked around Luigi's. We were trying to soak in every memory we had created in the place.

As we tossed our oil saturated paper plates and soda cans in the trash receptacle, Rayford initiated our call and response, "Tight to the end."

Clarence and I replied, "Tight to the end." Then all of a sudden Rayford and Clarence looked at each other and started laughing. Soon I felt Rayford's patronizing arm around my shoulders.

"Hey Clarence—Grey's come a long way since elementary school—huh?"

Clarence affirmed Rayford.

"And you know this!" I brushed Rayford's arm from around my shoulders, then reminded them both that I was the one with the car. A confident smirk emerged on my face as the mocking came to a screeching halt.

The weeks that followed our graduation celebration at Luigi's were filled with spending as much time together as we could. It was a balancing act for me as it had been in previous years to juggle time with Rayford and Clarence and my Davis Prep friends. In the end it all worked out fine as we all anticipated August as the month the next phase of our lives would begin. Rayford and a Davis Prep friend of mine name Kyle, would be heading to the military while Clarence, the rest of my

Davis Prep friends and I would be heading to colleges in different parts of the country.

The day before I left for college, I ran into Natalie at the grocery store. When we saw each other our faces lit up. As I walked toward her, though, something changed. Her eyes dropped and an expression of discomfort shone across her face. She had a couple of packages of diapers in her shopping cart.

"So, how have you been?" I asked with an awkward smile.

"Well, under the circumstances . . ." she pointed to the diapers in her shopping cart and continued, "I guess ok." I'm sure for a second or two I must have had a deer-in-the-headlights look on my face, but I quickly regained control.

"So, that's why you disappeared—huh?" Natalie sighed.

"Yup, that's exactly why I disappeared and that's exactly why I didn't, couldn't tell you what was going on. I was way too embarrassed. A part of me wanted to tell you everything. I wanted to tell you that I was leaving school and why, but when I looked into our homeroom and saw you, I got all emotional. All I could do was wave and then I left the school as soon as I could. I figured you'd come out when you realized that I wasn't coming in the room. Anyway, my parents were waiting for me in the car and it was probably best that I didn't irritate them anymore than I already had. Now that we're here talking though, and that I'm dealing with things better than I was, I'll fill you in.

"I got pregnant back in August. By November it was starting to get too hard to cover it up with baggy tops. So my parents decided to pull me out and get me a private tutor. I didn't walk with you guys, but at least I have my high school diploma. Mine just comes along with a baby. My parents are so disappointed in me. They had such plans for me. I had big plans for myself. Now, I don't know what I'm going to do. My parents want me to go to a local college. That wasn't their plan for me all these years, but everything has changed. They're trying to salvage what they can of a future for me, but I don't know anymore. I have this baby to take care of and that's it. What else can I do? The father of my baby wants to marry me but my father said, 'absolutely not.' He said he'd die first before he let his daughter marry the likes of Rufus."

Even though I wasn't interested in the rumors that had been passed around, I couldn't help but hear some of the talk. I shared a rumor with Natalie, "Well, there was some talk that Kevin James was the father of your baby. I guess the rumor only had the pregnant part right."

Natalie corrected me, "No, the rumor was right. Kevin is the father." Natalie rolled her eyes then shook her head in embarrassment and disgust. "My father calls any Black boy, who as much as puts his eyes on me, Rufus." Despite Natalie's sincere confession and apologetic tone, I couldn't hold back my laughter. I simply found the explanation of the name Rufus comical.

I apologized, "I'm sorry Natalie, for some reason I just found that really funny." Calming myself down and ridding my face of any and all signs of joking, I gently asked, "So, how are Woooofus and baby Wooooofus?" Natalie and I did a great deal of kidding around at Davis Prep, so after seeing and hearing my utter amusement over her father's seemingly mean spirited racial jab, a relief came over her that was refreshing and brought a broad bright smile to her face.

"George, I want you to know that I really missed you and I felt really bad that I didn't tell you what was going on."

I simply told Natalie, "No worries," and asked, "So, do you wuv Woooofus?"

Natalie's smile faded as she answered, "I don't know George. If it had to be anyone why couldn't it have been you?"

Caught a bit off guard I responded, "Me—why me?"

"I'm just talking crazy George. I don't know. I don't know anything right now. Hey—I have to get home. I am so glad we bumped into each other." Natalie gave me a warm hug and a kiss on the lips before saying goodbye. She pushed her cart to the express checkout lane where I watched her until she purchased her items and left. Somehow I knew that I would never see Natalie again.

# CHAPTER 12

# Observations of a Freshman

During my college years, I couldn't help but notice students who, at least, appeared to be perfectly matched with their chosen fields of study. From my vantage point, these students had incorporated their passions, personalities, interests and talents in the selection of their fields of study. In my eyes, these students had majors that were extensions of who they were, or at least who they believed themselves to be. Their interests in their major course work existed both in and out of their classrooms. Their areas of study excited them. Inside them there seemed to be an unforced and natural gravitation to matters directly and indirectly related to their major courses. Foreign to me, these students sought to learn and to be exposed to all they could with regard to their major studies. As I went through college, I never experienced pleasure and drive in my major. I only observed it in others, and my most frequent observations of this phenomenon were in my buddy Clarence. He was so personally connected to his field of study.

Clarence and I may have been attending the same school in Atlanta, Georgia, but Clarence was there with focus and purpose. Clarence was there to become a civic-minded preacher in the order of Martin

Luther King. He wanted to help guide humanity towards gentleness and tolerance. He was also bent on spreading the soul saving message of accepting Jesus Christ as one's personal savior. He wanted to lead people to hope through word and deed. He knew an academic education would enhance his plight, so he took his studies seriously. Knowing the wealth of Atlanta, with respect to its number of living civil rights activist legends, he sought to have audience, alliances and even friendships with as many of them as he could. I came face to face with this reality during the marches that were held in Atlanta each year on Martin Luther King's birthday. The major intent of the marches was to bring national attention to the quest of making King's birthday a national holiday.

The first march of our college career took place in our freshman year. The January 15th march started at the Atlanta University Center and concluded at the capitol building in down town Atlanta. It was at the capitol building where various civil rights leaders and civil rights minded people addressed the gathered crowd. At eighteen years of age, my hometown friend, Clarence Davenport was numbered among the day's speakers. He shared a few words of prayer for the ending of the apartheid in South Africa and a plea to free Nelson Mandela from his imprisonment in Cape Town, South Africa. At the podium, Clarence was in the company of Coretta Scott King, Ralph Abernathy, Julian Bond, Maynard Jackson and Stevie Wonder to name a few. He wasn't simply a student majoring in religion and political science. He was so much more.

The more I reminisced on those days the more admiration for Clarence developed in me. I discretely turned to him as he sat on my porch sipping his glass of lemonade. I smiled to myself until the dread of my lack of personal direction swept it away. Why was I so clueless and void of personal direction in college, and why was I so clueless and void of personal direction in my adult life? On the porch, I sat bound by sadness.

As I struggled to mask my mood change, Clarence, out of all things to say, brought up the MLK marches.

"Hey Grey, you remember the marches to the Capitol in Atlanta on King's birthdays? Man—I loved every one of them."

Continuing to shield my mood change, I brought an insincere smile to my face and answered, "Yeah—I remember them Clarence. I marched, but you were truly a part of them—elbow-to-elbow with the likes of Coretta Scott King and Ralph Abernathy. I saw you. Every year you were like a little King." Hearing this, Rayford's expression turned to one of particular interest.

"So, what's this I hear Clarence? Back in the day you were fighting the fight alongside Coretta Scott King and Ralph Abernathy?"

"No, no—hold on Rayford, it wasn't all that. I was just lucky enough to be asked to give prayers at the rallies that followed the MLK birthday marches. I was no mover and shaker. I was just a young man who was overcome with happiness and gratefulness to have been in the company of such great people."

Rayford just smiled and quietly added, "I hear you bro. Well, you know I did my thing too to help get King's birthday to be a national holiday." Ignorant to what Rayford's contribution might have been I took the bait.

"And what did you do? You guys had marches in the army?"

Taking full advantage of the attention, Rayford slowly and deliberately answered, "No—brotha Grey, that wasn't my style. I—chose a more personal route. I wrote to my congressman." Totally impressed, both Clarence and I nodded our heads with a look of astonished approval. Rayford, quite pleased and full of himself simply and slowly turned his eyes away from us to the street where he was excited to see a good looking woman walking by.

"Man—this neighborhood always had the finest women." Shaking our heads at Rayford, Clarence and I started laughing which got Rayford laughing as well. Consequently my demons were warded off and I was light-hearted again. Momentarily relieved of my depressed state, I began to privately reminisce on other memories of our first year in college.

# CHAPTER 13

# The Pastor's Daughter

After a wonderful summer break following our freshman year of college, Clarence and I returned to school in late August. The first week of classes was typical. The professors handed out syllabi and informed us of the text books that would be needed for their classes. Most professors kept the first day pretty general, but a few taught intense lessons and assigned homework from the text books they, only minutes earlier, had instructed us to obtain. I never saw the logic of such practices.

At the end of the week Clarence and I headed to the bookstore. We were both in good spirits. As we walked, we hoped to get all our books at one time. Having to go back to the bookstore more than once was simply not desirable. The crowds at the beginning of the semester are always bad and the lines are incredibly long. Sometimes the lines are even out the door just to get into the bookstore. Once you get in and find the books you're looking for, then you have to stand on another line to pay for the books. During the summer we tried to save enough money to take care of our various school expenses for both semesters. So, we really hoped that the cost of our books wouldn't put too much of a strain on our summer savings. Books, although, the largest expense, were not our only expense.

As it turned out, the hope of purchasing every book we needed in one shopping day was dashed. Some of the books we needed had already been sold and others were still on order having yet not arrived at the bookstore. Also dashed was any hope we had of our books being even moderately priced. Having purchased the books we needed that were in stock, we left the bookstore with plans to return the following week.

Standing on the corner in front of the bookstore, I grumbled my unhappiness with the game that I felt was being played with college students and the purchasing of their text books.

"You know I was going to buy a used calculus book from a guy who took it last semester, but today in class the instructor informed us that we would need edition 5 as opposed to edition 4. What could possibly be different between these two books? Math doesn't change! It's all a racket! It's all a financial racket and I hate it."

Clarence cut in, "Man—if the devil ain't running this world I don't know who is."

"I know exactly what you're saying Clarence. It's all about the almighty dollar. That's why I'm not on the meal plan this semester."

With a wrinkled brow Clarence turned to me and asked me how I planned on eating. Without waiting for my answer he responded, "You see—me—I need the meal plan. I need to eat three meals a day. I actually wish the meal plan included four meals. I'd make every one of them." With a bit of a chuckle I assured Clarence that I thought through my decision very carefully.

"My situation is different from yours Clarence. The meal plan just doesn't work for me. Last semester I wasted alot of money being on the meal plan. Second semester I lived off campus and it was a pain trying to get to the cafeteria before it closed. I missed way too many meals. Too many times I ended up paying double for one meal. When I missed a meal that was prepaid, I still had to go and find food and pay for it. This year, I'm off campus again, but I'm not going to pay for the meal plan. I'm in the driver's seat! If I'm on campus when a meal is being served, I'll pay for it out of my pocket. But, if I'm not on or near campus, I'll just reach in that same pocket and buy my meal at some place closer to where I happen to be—one meal, one price. You see what I'm saying?"

Clarence understood and summed things up in a preacher's style similar to Martin Luther King.

"I may not join you in your forgoing of the meal plan, but as a people we will both dine, filling our bellies and giving thanks to the Almighty for his abundant grace and mercy." Gleaming from his performance he smiled proudly.

Trying to hide my smile, I shook my head and told him, "Shut up . . . just shut up."

As Clarence and I crossed the street he saw one of his friends a few yards ahead of us. He called to her. She spotted him and as a big smile came over her face she crossed the street to where we were standing. She and Clarence hugged.

"Where are you headed Reverend Clarence—prayer meetin'?"

"Ha, ha very funny Denise, are you still stripping at that club downtown?" My mouth opened and my eyes grew wide.

Denise quickly announced a truce, "Ok, ok I know I started this." She looked at me and quite emphatically told me that she was no stripper but that she was a dance major on a dance scholarship. Amused, I laughed and reassured her that I knew that she and Clarence were just playing around. Kidding aside, Denise, once again, asked Clarence where he was going but this time without adding any of her spicy input. It was news to me but Clarence told her that he was headed to the library and asked her if she wanted to join him. Denise answered that she wanted to go and further added that the library was, in fact, where she was headed.

Silently I watched these two make their plans. Clarence and I were supposed to be with his pastor's daughter at her dormitory getting ready to show her around the Atlanta University (AU) Center: an appointment I had no problem missing. Earlier in the week, Clarence's pastor cornered Clarence into committing to spend time with his daughter. The pastor's daughter was a freshman and he wanted to arrange some assurances that his daughter would have a watchful eye over her as she adjusted to college life away from home. The cornering took place via a three-way telephone call that was strategically set up by the pastor. The three parties were Clarence, the pastor's daughter, and the pastor. The pastor must have felt that having his daughter on the phone would decrease any chances of Clarence saying no. Clarence had a soft heart and the pastor knew it. More to the point, though, Clarence's pastor had every trust in Clarence. He knew he could trust Clarence with his baby girl. What the pastor didn't know, however, was that any guy could be trusted with his baby girl. She was neither a pleasure on the nerves nor upon the eyes. Having made the commitment, Clarence made me promise to come along. The pastor's daughter had more than a little crush on him and he didn't want to give her any ideas that would encourage her affection toward him.

As the memory of his commitment dawned on him, Clarence spoke disappointingly to Denise, "Ahh man, I can't go Denise. Grey and I have something we have to do."

Denise responded with a noticeable degree of disappointment sweetened, however, by her genuine good nature, "Hey it's alright. We'll have plenty of time to go to the library. You and Grey . . ." Denise paused, and then continued, glancing over to me, "I guess this is Grey. Go and do what you have to do." I seized the opportunity to confirm her assumption.

"Yes, hi, my name is George Grey."

Denise politely responded, "Hi George, I'm Denise. I'm Glad to meet you."

With an embarrassed, little boy's grin on his face, Clarence simply said, "Oops—my bad."

I guess feeling awkward about having not introduced us, Clarence abruptly changed the subject. He brought up my meal plan decision.

"Hey Denise, can you believe Grey, I mean George, he isn't on the meal plan?" A bit confused over the randomness of the question, Denise went with the flow and asked me how I planned to eat. I told her the same thing I told Clarence. Then out of the blue, she offered me her hot plate. As silly as it may sound, I never thought about using a hot plate.

Denise restated her offer, "I'm serious George if you want to have my hot plate you're more than welcome to have it."

From the moment I watched and listened to the interaction between Clarence and Denise I could tell that she was a special kind of person: the offering of her hot plate sealed my opinion. I told her I would love to have the plate and that I'd get it from her sometime over the weekend. I thanked her over and over again. My friendship with Denise started that day and in the days, weeks and months that followed we got to be better friends. It was as though we had been friends for years.

After parting company with Denise, Clarence and I started making our way to Spelman College. Spelman is the all-girl college of the AU Center. Once we arrived at Spelman's entry gate we walked to the security shack and surrendered our school IDs to the security officer. Once the officer cleared our IDs as authentic and took temporary possession of them, we were given approval to enter the quite lovely, I might add, campus. On the grounds we headed for Abbey Hall. We walked along the paved drive-route which curved and branched throughout the campus giving access to every dormitory. Abbey Hall, one of the dormitories, was the main freshman dormitory and consequently the residence of Angela, Clarence's pastor's daughter.

When Clarence and I arrived at Abbey Hall we went to the front desk to have Angela paged. Within moments the page was made. We stood and waited. We were confident that she was in the dormitory because our visit was preplanned. In a short few minutes Angela was in the lobby looking around for the person or persons who had paged her. Her face displayed a most distasteful scowl. The scowl, however, turned to pure joy when her eyes caught sight of Clarence. When Angela's eyes caught sight of me she gave me a nasty rolling of the eyes.

Noticing Angela's eyes rolling and my responsive facial expression Clarence asked, "Do you two know each other?" I told Clarence that Angela and I had met at the youth extravaganza at Mount Carmel back home. Mount Carmel was Clarence's and Angela's church. Angela's father was the founding pastor.

With no more tact than she had at the youth extravaganza, Angela blurted out, "Yeah, this is the boy who tried to talk to me in my daddy's church!"

Learning of Angela's slant on what happened, I answered back, "Talk to you? I wasn't trying to talk to you. The purpose of the youth extravaganza was to get to know people. The event coordinators told us to group ourselves and to get to know the people in our group. You were next to me so I asked you if you wanted to be in my group."

"Please boy, you were trying to talk to me. Why would I want to be in your group?" Dumfounded I just stood with my mouth open wondering how anyone could be so ignorant.

To break the tension Clarence, interrupted, "Hey Angela, how's dorm life?" Once again entirely focused on Clarence, a smile reemerged on Angela's face and she gave Clarence a big hug. Clarence wasn't rude. He hugged her back. I think in some way he enjoyed the hug. At the very least

I believe he found it flattering. Clarence had to initiate the breaking of the hug, though. I thought he did a good job of it. It wasn't too abrupt. It was just right. Having not gotten an answer to his question, Clarence asked again, "So, how's dorm life?" Angela wrinkled her nose, but not in a cute girl sort of way. It resembled more of the way a bull's nose wrinkles when he's about to charge someone.

"I don't think I'm going to make it with my roommate. This girl is irritating."

With a smile and a bit of a laugh Clarence asked, "Already? C'mon now Angela, give it some time."

With an attitude Angela simply said, "I'm just saying, this girl better stay out of my business if she knows what's good for her." Keeping things light Clarence kept his good nature.

"Alright, so do you want a tour of the AU Center?"

Clarence's calming smile soothed Angela and without hesitation she answered, "Yup, I sure do!"

Looking over to me then back at Clarence, Angela asked with a bit of a snarl, "Is he going?"

Clarence remained upbeat and simply said, "Girl, you are too much. Everybody's going. C'mon, let's go!" With that we were out of Abbey Hall, off of the campus and engaged in the tour of the center. Angela's, behavior was surprising almost civilized. All in all it ended up being a decently uneventful, few hours.

# CHAPTER 14

# *Plan B*

The semester progressed into November and Mid-Terms were upon us. One Saturday, with intentions to study for my upcoming tests, I walked to the library. The cooler temperatures and the browning leaves on the trees brought the reality and anticipation of Thanksgiving to mind. Because of cost concerns I wouldn't be making the trip home for Thanksgiving, but that didn't stop me from entertaining fond memories of past Thanksgivings with my family. In the library I found a nice quiet spot to study. I tried my best to focus on studying but my Thanksgiving memories became a stumbling block. I left the library to readjust my priorities. I stood and did a little pacing on the landing between the doors of the library and the steps.

There was a bit of a chill in the air and college students were everywhere. Some were leaving the library, others were arriving and still others were, as I was, outside on a break.

"Whatcha doing?" Startled, I jerked my head toward the voice. It was Denise.

"Man—where did you come from?" In her friendly joking way, Denise said she had been there beside me the whole time and that she was trying to wait for me to notice her.

"Yeah—right," I responded. She laughed.

"So—Mr. Grey are you going home for Thanksgiving this year?"

"No, I can't afford to go home for Thanksgiving and then follow that with a trip home for Christmas. How about you? Are you going home for Thanksgiving?"

"Yup, I'm going. La Grange is close enough to Atlanta so I can go home pretty much whenever I want." Not wanting to seem like a Thanksgiving orphan, I shared with Denise that a cousin of mine in Durham, North Carolina had invited Clarence and me to spend Thanksgiving break at her house. With a look of interest, Denise asked if I were going to take my cousin up on her offer.

For some reason the look in Denise's eyes brought the question, "Why not?" for the first time to my mind. My cousin had truly invited Clarence and me. I had just never entertained the idea. I looked at Denise.

"You know something? I just might go. I just might . . ."

In a peaceful voice Denise encouraged me, "I think you should George."

Later on that evening I went to Clarence's dorm room to ask him about the idea of going to Durham for Thanksgiving.

All Clarence said was, "Amen and amen. When do we leave?" I told him that I'd call my cousin later on that night to firm things up, but really interested in the idea he urged me saying, "No Grey, call your cousin now. I need to know if I'm going to be eating a meal-plan Thanksgiving dinner or a home cooked one." I couldn't argue with what I was hearing, so I called my cousin from the hall phone in Clarence's dormitory. After getting off the phone with my cousin, Clarence and I had confirmed accommodations for Thanksgiving in Durham, North Carolina. We didn't discuss how we would exactly get there, though. We put that bit of planning off until after Mid-Terms.

Between the two of us I had the last Mid-Term. It was over at 9am the Wednesday before Thanksgiving. After finishing the test I got with Clarence to discuss our mode of transportation. We decided to rent a car. We had never done it before, but there were plenty of things we had never done before that we ended up doing, so renting a car didn't seem like an insurmountable task. With no reason to find to foil that idea, we made the decision and plan to rent the car by noon, drive it back to campus, get packed and be on the road by 5:00pm. I remembered seeing a car rental place on International Boulevard the last time I was downtown. Whether it was Avis, Budget Rental or some other rental company, I wasn't sure, it didn't matter. We just needed a car.

Close to campus, we boarded the first of two city buses. We each handed fifty cents, the single person fare, to the bus driver. Needing to catch a second bus, we each requested a transfer card. We arrived at the car rental place with plenty of time to make our schedule. We sat for a moment or two waiting for the availability of a rental agent. With not too long of a wait we were called to the desk of an agent who had concluded business with an earlier customer. In less time than we spent waiting to speak to an agent we were walking out of the car rental place empty handed, knowing from that moment on, the cruel realities of not owning a credit card.

With his spirits and chin high, Martin Luther Clarence shared, "If the good Lord closes one door, he'll open another. I feel, in my spirit, the draft of a wind coming from the open door at the Greyhound bus station." We broke out into laughter as we made our way to the Greyhound station on Piedmont Avenue. Reaching the bus station we approached the information desk to inquire about buses departing for Durham. The clerk informed us that one was about to leave and the next and last one, that day, would be departing at 2:30 PM. It was already noon, but we felt we could pull off making the 2:30 bus, so looking at each other we nodded in unspoken agreement, told the clerk that we'd see her soon then hurriedly left the station.

Taking the two-bus route back to campus was out of the question. The reasonable possibility of having to wait as much as twenty minutes per bus would in no way serve our end, so we set out running back to campus. Unlike the buses, we could take a direct and mandatory stop free route back to campus. As long as our bodies could remain in running motion we had a chance. Clarence and I were both athletes and were similarly built. The sum of the parts of two athletes is not, however, always equal.

We started our run. I kept up as best I could. The manner in which Clarence ran was different from the way I ran. His speed, focus and control were unbelievable. I could never begin to match his skill. It was obvious to me that he was holding back. I was a strong runner but it was only because I trained hard. My hard training was the reason for my athletic success. I was never the leader of the pack or ever in the finishing top five, though. I was satisfied to fill the coaches' basic requirements. My high school football achievements were a direct result of me realizing my abilities and wisely working with them. As Clarence and I ran back to campus, I can only hope that I looked good while I ran alongside him. Looking good in a physical activity was always important to me.

We continued our run making the last right turn before the left onto Northside Drive. This was probably the widest street in Atlanta, with the exception of I-75/85 or even I-20. We traveled on Northside with the traffic. Just ahead we knew there would be a major incline. Up to this point the run was relatively flat, with some hills going our way—downward. Thanks to Clarence for slowing down for most of the run, we managed to stay together. At the incline I pushed with everything I had. We made it onto

Fair Street. My college apartment was on Fair and not a moment too soon did we arrive at the entrance to the complex. Clarence still had a ways to go to get to his dorm room on campus.

Bent over and caught up in exhaustion, my hands were on my knees.

My eyes facing the pavement, I managed, while slowly turning to Clarence to ask, "Clarence, are you going to be able to get to your dorm, pack and get back here in thirty minutes?" Still slowly turning toward him, I didn't hear him answer. I wondered if he was Ok. Finally turned in the direction where I expected him to be, I didn't see him. I lifted my head. Sweat ran down my forehead into my eyes. I could hardly see. Wiping my brow still bent over and breathing hard, my vision cleared. In that moment it had become evident why Clarence had not responded. He was well on his way. Not only did he not break stride, but his speed seemed to have elevated from what the two of us had previously maintained. He seemed to have the stride of Secretariat in 1973 at the Belmont. He had his hand in the air signaling his assurance that he'd be back within a time that wouldn't hamper our travel plans. It was a sight to see.

Clarence came back, with a tightly packed garment bag and a shoulder bag. I had the same. I was standing out at the curb where, just thirty minutes earlier, we parted company. Everything up to that point had worked according to the layout of our plan B. Uncertain about how to get back down town, God put someone in our path. The girlfriend of one of my school mates showed up and offered us a ride. Clarence and I can be somewhat cavalier and independent to a fault; our intentions were to get ourselves, without assistance, back to the bus station but I believe God used my schoolmate's girlfriend to help teach Clarence and me the lesson that although independence is fine, every once in a while getting help and accepting it from people is a good thing. There are times and situations when the aid of another is simply smart, beneficial and downright necessary.

We made the bus in enough time to casually purchase our tickets and board our bus to Durham. We had a great time sharing Thanksgiving with my cousin. Clarence ate like there was no tomorrow.

# CHAPTER 15

# Godsend

In our junior year of college, Clarence and I celebrated Thanksgiving in Virginia with Rayford. Rayford was on leave from the army. He contacted Clarence and me and told us to meet him in Portsmouth, Virginia at his great aunt's house. We hadn't seen Rayford in a long while so we were more than happy to make the trip.

As it turned out we drove to Virginia with two of Clarence's dorm mates—Russell and Keith. The owner of the car, Russell, was from Virginia Beach. He was looking for people to help offload the cost of gas and burden of driving. He owned a white, late-model, 8 cylinder gas guzzling Mercury Cougar. He had already secured one paying companion and was looking for two others. After a conversation with Clarence, the two open spots became Clarence's and mine.

With the car all packed with everyone's luggage, we left late afternoon on the Wednesday before Thanksgiving. Russell took the first leg of the trip. Night came fast. I was out like a light until, in a semi-sleep, drowsy state, I noticed the car was not moving and that Russell was talking to a light. Rubbing my eyes and stretching, I fully awoke and realized that the light to which Russell was talking had a police officer behind it. Russell had been pulled over for speeding. I was in the back seat with Keith.

Keith whispered to me, "Russell doesn't have the registration card for his car but before the cop walked up, Russell told us not to worry because he had his Virginia driver's license." I sank in my seat hoping we'd only be locked up and not beaten.

I looked at Keith and whispered back, "Where are we?"

Continuing to whisper Keith answered, "South Carolina."

Leaning toward Keith, I whispered even softer, "I can't tell you what a relief it is to know that no-registration-having Russell is in dialogue with a good-ole-boy, southern cop with three other Black males in his car of which two are whispering in the back seat." Keith snickered and told me not to worry reminding me that Russell had his Virginia license. Shaking my head in comical disbelief, I whispered back to Keith, "Oh that's right. I feel so much better now."

Suddenly the flashlight that had been shone in Russell's face was in mine, then Keith's face.

"Su'm back there wrong?"

In unison we responded, "No, sir." The officer instructed Russell to exit the car. The two walked to the officer's squad car. Shortly after, Russell returned to his car with only a speeding ticket. We were amazed—happy—but amazed. Russell drove until the police officer passed us. I'm sure he was feeling disappointed and maybe even a little embarrassed, from having gotten the speeding ticket. Shortly after the officer drove by, Russell pulled to the shoulder of the road, turned to Keith and spoke the first words since informing us that he was only given a speeding ticket.

"This is my car. It's your turn to drive." Understanding the circumstances and Russell's personality, Keith, Clarence and I contained our impulse to laugh and to poke fun at Russell's rude manner. Keith, having been ordered to drive, simply got out of the car and took over as the new driver.

We were making good time and the memory of our encounter with the South Carolina officer was fading when suddenly the cabin of the car was flooded with rotating red, white and blue lights. Once again we were being pulled over by another police officer. We were in North Carolina. This police officer was similar to the previous one. He was white and spoke with a thick southern accent: an accent reminiscent of television accounts of law officials who abuse Black people. Once again, however, the only ticket written was for speeding. The next driver was Clarence.

Clarence was a good driver. There wouldn't be any incidences of tickets on his leg of the trip. He was a conservative and cool driver who didn't take chances and was always mindful of doing the right thing. I knew we were safe. We made it out of North Carolina and into Virginia as eventless as I had predicted. About twenty minutes into Virginia, however, it happened. Clarence was pulled over for speeding and just like Russell and Keith, he received a speeding ticket. Clarence had crossed the burning sands into the fraternity of the ticketed. It was my turn to drive. It was my job to bring our trip to an end without induction into the fraternity.

I took the wheel along with the responsibility to take advantage of a teaching opportunity for the fraternal order of the ticketed. I wanted them to pay close attention to my techniques of driving while being fully observant of the need to manipulate the environment. I tried to demonstrate, that when driving, one doesn't simply sit and steer. The driving environment changes and while the vehicle is in one's charge, it is the responsibility of the one in charge to take the opportunities as they come to modify his driving tactics to optimize results. At times there are no options but to travel the speed limit. I could tell they were ready to learn; I was ready to teach.

Class was in session. I had come under a set of circumstances which deemed it necessary to travel the speed limit. I reduced my speed to under the speed limit and proceeded with the driver education. It was 2 O'clock in the morning. We were well into Virginia. I told the fraternity boys that it would not be long before we got to Virginia Beach. Unseen before, I noticed a car out of my rear view mirror. There hadn't been any cars on the road for miles. Based on the rate at which the car behind us was gaining on me, it was clear its driver was traveling well above the speed limit. He passed by in a blur.

Acknowledging another teaching opportunity, I spoke aloud, "Fellas, there's my goat. Here's a chance to make some good time. I'll follow this car. If a cop is around, he'll stop the goat, I'll slow down and we'll be spared any interruptions." My goat was good for a couple of miles. But after about three minutes he had accelerated far out of my sight. I was speeding without my goat. My environment changed. I, in turn, began to break my speed. As I was slowing down, I looked into my rear view mirror and saw the bright red, white and blue lights spinning around. The only thing left was for me to talk my way out of the ticket or be inducted as the last inductee into the fraternity of the ticketed.

Using the squad car's loud speaker, the police officer instructed me to exit the car and to join him in his car. He sat and waited for my compliance. Seated in his car, in a southern drawl, similar to the prior three police officers, the officer who stopped me asked if I knew that I was traveling at 72 miles an hour in a 60 miles per hour speed zone.

"I don't believe I was going that fast," I replied.

He merely said, "Yep," as he began to write my ticket. He asked me for my driver's license and nothing else. In a matter of minutes I was asked to sign the ticket.

In response I asked, "What if I don't sign?"

As cool as he could be he responded in a quite matter of fact manner, "Well son, you and I will be spending a lot of time together."

Without hesitation I asked one last question, "Where do I sign?"

I got back in the car and before we knew it we were in Virginia Beach. We dropped Keith off at his brother's house then drove, only minutes away, to Russell's parents' house where Clarence and I got a few hours of sleep before Russell drove us to Rayford's aunt's house in Portsmouth.

When we drove up Rayford was outside. It had been a while since the three of us were together. After Clarence and I greeted Rayford, Rayford paused. Staring at us a smile came to his face.

"Tight to the end," to which Clarence and I responded, "Tight to the end." I can't express in words the feeling that welled up in me but from the expressions on Rayford and Clarence's faces, I believe they experienced the same emotion.

Rayford broke the silence, "Come on and meet my people."

Meeting Rayford's southern relatives was a bit of a shock. Although undetected in his form of speech, Rayford comes from country stock. His father and his father's side of the family are originally from rural South Carolina. Their brand of English was like a foreign language to Clarence and me. As foreign as their speech was, I must say that I never had so much fun among people I couldn't understand as I did that Thanksgiving. Rayford's relatives seemed to be people who were determined to not allow the sad things of life keep them from enjoying the precious things in life. It was clear that Rayford had honestly inherited their style of life.

I doubt if any two friends were as different as Rayford and I were, but ever since the day I met him in the woods, he has inspired me. My free spirited friend could always set a charge in me. The charge wasn't always positive, but whether it was a positive or negative it always seemed to serve a benefit for me in the end. Rayford was my Godsend.

# CHAPTER 16

# *Transformation*

The story of the ugly duckling blossoming into a beautiful swan was no better put before my eyes and ears than it was back in September. I had decided to blow off some time so I walked to West End Mall. West End Mall was a common hang out for the students of the AU Center. It wasn't a large or particularly attractive mall but it was close in proximity to the Center's schools and as such was frequented by the students of the center. Arriving at the mall, I walked in. With Barely two steps in the mall I was immediately captivated by the sight of one of the shapeliest females I had ever seen. I paused briefly to savor the fleeting moment. Within moments she was gone. She entered one of the mall shops just ahead of me. The shop was along the entry corridor of the mall. As I proceeded along the entry corridor I anticipated walking by the shop in hopes of getting a better view of her and hopefully her face. As I neared the shop I slowed down and, as nonchalantly as I could, I peered over at the shop. It was like she disappeared. I didn't see her anywhere. Staying cool and collected I cut my losses and proceeded past the shop.

Suddenly from behind me I heard my name called, "Grey!" Clarence was the only one who called me Grey in Atlanta but the voice that called my name was clearly not his. The voice carrying my name was a female voice. I turned around. The girl that I had just been looking for was standing at the entrance of the shop looking in my direction. I knew it was she. The contour of her jeans bore undeniable witness to that fact.

Cautiously excited, I pointed to my chest and mouthed, "Me?"

Sweetly she replied, "I don't see anybody else, do you?" Like an idiot I looked around. She started to laugh. "You don't know who I am, do you?" I shook my head then finally started walking toward her. I struggled to figure out who this beauty of a girl was. Not only did she know me but she knew what they called me back at home as well.

Arriving and stopping just in front of her, a name came to mind, but the name didn't quite agree with the person who initiated the contact I was eagerly obliging.

Tentatively I asked—"Angela?"

With a smile she responded, "Oh, so you do know me."

Not knowing quite what to say, I stuttered. "You . . . you're different. This is the first time I've ever been around you and you were nice to me. Don't get me wrong. I'm not complaining. It's just different and . . ."

"And what George?"

"Well, you, ummm . . . you look different. You look nice . . . really, really nice." As I stood, I struggled to get my mind to accept the fact that the girl who put the original "s" in scowl was now speaking to me with: the sweetest of tones, a smile as warm as southern comfort and a figure to put Josephine Baker to shame. Angela coyly giggled.

"Yes, I've gone through some changes since we last saw each other. I was a mess George. My personality was horrible. My attitude was horrible and I looked horrible in the mirror. I don't know if Clarence told you but I sat out my second semester; it was actually encouraged by the Provost. I got into a fight with my roommate . . . you remember the one I told you and Clarence about? Well, I lost it and we went to blows. Somehow news of the fight made its way to the Provost's ears. I wasn't told not to come back, but as I was saying, I was encouraged to take a little break. A call was also made to my parents leaving them with the same encouragement. The fight happened in early December. I finished out the semester and braced myself to face my parents. They drove down to pick me up. The drive back home was terrible. There was so much arguing. I had developed a really bad don't care attitude. My parents said that they didn't even know who I was anymore.

"One weekend at home in January, I was in the park. My parents were driving me up the wall. I needed some space so I put on my coat and went for a walk. I ended up in Luther Park. Well, once I got to the park, I don't know, I ended up sitting down at a picnic table that was situated in a dark corner of one of the pavilions. Sitting there shivering, this old man came up to me. I was ready to give him some classic attitude but there was something about him that quieted me. I can't explain it. With a gentle smile he stood and looked at me as I sat at the picnic table.

Then he asked, 'Now, why is such a pretty girl sitting in the dark?'

George, he didn't come off like a dirty old man trying to make a play. It was different. The man was different, like no one I have ever met. I didn't answer his question but his question penetrated me. That man wanted to know why a pretty girl, me George, was sitting in the cold. I can't remember the last time someone called me pretty." I saw tears form in the corners of Angela's eyes. My heart sank. She wiped them away with the back of her hand, and then apologized. "I'm sorry George. I've been through so much." Gathering herself, she laughed aloud. It wasn't a festive laugh though. Under the impression that she shared more than what the moment called for, she set her mind to correct her course. "George, I apologize again, I know you have better ways of spending your time at the mall then standing here listening to me talk and watching me cry. I'm going to let you go. Thanks for listening. You were always a sweet guy I just couldn't appreciate it before and wasn't able to admit it."

Touched by what I had seen and heard, I just stood for a moment looking at Angela. Then finally I crossed my arms and began to speak.

"So—you're just going to leave a brother hanging without knowing the end of the story?"

With quizzical pleasure Angela responded, "You seriously want to hear more?"

"You're in a park, freezing your butt off in the middle of January. A strange old man walks up to you. You don't give him attitude. He compliments you, and again you don't give him attitude or go off on him, but instead you're soothed by it all, and you want to know if I'm serious about wanting to know what happened next?" Angela burst into laughter.

"George, you are crazy! Hey—what are you doing after you leave the mall?"

"Nothing, I was just going to go back to campus."

"Ok, look, I'll wait for you around here and when you're done shopping we'll walk to Mrs. Winner's on the way back to your campus. I'll buy you a two piece meal for being such a good sport and tell you the rest of my story on the way there—ok? Oh wait—do you even like Mrs. Winner's chicken? I shouldn't assume you like it."

"I love Mrs. Winner's chicken and to be honest, I just came to the mall to walk around so, if you're good with leaving now, let's go."

With no reason to stay at the mall, Angela and I left and almost as soon as the mall door closed behind us I asked, "Ok Angela, what happened next?"

With a very pleasant look on her face she picked up where she left off, "Well, as I said, I didn't answer his question. I was quiet. That is all I could do to manage the impact of his compliment. He asked me if he could sit down with me. I just shrugged my shoulders. He sat across the table from me George and again, I can't explain it but there was nothing frightening about him. In fact there was like a peace about him that touched me. Soon after he sat down he asked me, 'How did such a pretty girl loose her light?' Just like the other question, this new question penetrated me but it penetrated deeper and it wasn't the fact of him calling me pretty that consumed me, it was the part about the light. He wanted to know how I lost my light. George it was like this man knew me. It was like I couldn't hide from him even if I tried. I asked him why he asked me those two questions. Real gently he answered me. He said, 'Because you'll soar with the eagles if you hear, from your own voice. Hearing yourself answer, you'll begin to take flight.' I didn't understand him. Then he put his hand over my hands that were placed one over the other on table and asked, 'Now why is such a pretty girl sitting in the cold?' My chest felt heavy and I couldn't breathe at first. Then as a tear fell from my eye I told him that it was because I was lost. I felt his hand protectively tighten over my hands. Then he asked, 'How did such a pretty girl lose her way?' I just stared blankly until tears began streaming down my face. Then I answered him, 'Because all being a preacher's kid gets you is misery, unfair expectations and cruel judgment from people who know that your father is a preacher.' Then through tears and sniffing I asked the old man why he kept calling me pretty. He looked at me with no hesitation and said, 'Because you are. You don't recognize it because you stopped seeing it, and you stopped seeing it because you stopped feeling it.' He asked his last question. 'Can a person see, in a dark place, without a light?' I answered him, 'No.' 'Then,' he said, 'leave this dark place you're in and seek again the light. He's waiting for your return and wants to bless you richly.' After that he stood up, gently touched me on the top of my head and walked away.

"I was in fog when he left. Beginning to get really cold I got up, walked home, went to my room and went to bed. I woke up the next morning just before sunrise. I lay in my bed playing back the questions the old man asked me and my answers. Then suddenly the fog in my mind cleared. God made me pretty from the inside out. But just like anybody else I needed light to see it. Since my bad reactions to people who were hurting me led me away from the light, I got lost and mean. But thanks to that man, who I know God sent, I realized that I didn't want to be lost and mean anymore. I knew Jesus was waiting for me to return to him so he could rescue me. I rededicated my life to Christ, started eating right and exercising. When my parents saw the change in me they were so happy. When I told them that I wanted to go back to school, they didn't hesitate to help me get things in order to return the following fall semester. So here I am George, a new, no longer lost and joy-filled woman." I don't think I had ever heard a personal testimony from anyone that I knew that moved me as much as Angela's testimony.

Arriving at Mrs. Winner's, I couldn't bring myself to accept Angela's offer to buy me a two piece chicken basket, so I ordered and paid for both of our orders. She had given me so much in sharing her story, her testimony; I wanted to give something to her.

We ate in the restaurant and talked each other's heads off. It was a wonderful day.

A day or two after meeting the new Angela, Clarence and I were on the bus heading to the Omni Hotel and mall downtown. We wanted to walk around and maybe take in a movie.

Sitting on the bus I asked, "Did you know that Angela sat out last semester?"

"Yeah, her father told me. How did you find out?" I told Clarence that I ran into her a couple of days ago. With a smile on his face he turned to me and said, "She's not the same girl is she? The beast turned into a beauty—huh?" I laughed.

"You're not lying, but it was mostly her personality. Don't get me wrong now, with the weight she lost and the way she looks in her cloths, she's turning heads now, but the personality change is phenomenal, don't you think?" Clarence nodded his head.

"Yeah, it really is. She got her spiritual life on track. Hey, 'There's wonder working power in the blood of the lamb,' just like Lewis E. Jones wrote."

Contemplative, I nodded and replied, "Amen brother."

Fully aware of how Angela felt about Clarence the previous fall semester I asked, "So, is anything going to happen between you two?" Clarence just laughed.

"No, my eye isn't on Angela. It's on this girl I just met at the civic conference I attended last weekend. I was going to bring it up before you started talking about Angela. We were in a workshop together. I'm probably going to sound crazy, but I think she's the one I've been looking for all my life. I'm going to see her again next weekend. There's another conference. When I leave next weekend's conference I plan to have her phone number." I didn't say a word. I just sat quietly with a grin on my face. Clarence reassured me, "Ok, you watch. You just watch." We joked around for the remainder of time until arriving at the Omni.

Later on that week I went to Spelman with a few friends. We didn't have any purpose for going other than to be on the all-girl campus. One of my friends suggested that we go to McAlpine. McAlpine was the upper classman dormitory where his cousin stayed. As we walked to the dormitory I heard my name called. It was Angela. She was walking to the campus bookstore. Gesturing, she invited me to join her. With not even a degree of shame I bid my friends a fond adieu and joined her. At that time I didn't have any ideas or notions of having a dating relationship with

Angela, but after that day she and I began spending more and more time together. After a while we became really good friends and in mid-January, about four months later, we started dating.

The crush she had on Clarence, for some reason, left with the emergence of the new Angela. Neither she nor I understood why it faded but based on the good times and affection we shared for one another, it was clear that neither one of us regarded it with any concern.

# CHAPTER 17

# The Surrogate

Despite fond memories of moments during my college career of which Angela was the reason for most, at no time during those years did I feel that I was on track or comfortable with my life. My selected major was one of high regard. It was one the general public respected and one the evolving economy was poised to continue to monetarily reward. Unfortunately for me, however, my major wasn't one that inspired interest in me and because I spent no time evaluating who I was, who and what I wanted to be, and what major or majors were better suited for me, I was emotionally unengaged in college. As I matriculated, uninspired, through my major course work, feelings of being a guest at the party of my life were never far from me. Memorable college moments, although I will always treasure them, were fleeting and their end was always dreaded because I knew I had to return to the reality of my interest-void major.

What was I living? I was certainly not living my life. I was simply going through the motions. My performance in my classes was good but only because my fundamental understanding of the purpose of school was to earn high grades. College, for me, was a mechanical progression much the same as my progression from kindergarten to twelfth grade; after successfully completing one year of school, the next year began with no bearing or relation to anything personally gripping. Good or bad and possibly good and bad, I tended to stick with things in which I had become involved. Consequently I stayed the course of following my initial plan for my college studies and kept my major.

As things turned out I was offered and I accepted a good paying job which had direct correlation to my major field of study. All of this was completed within the last month or so before I graduated. I knew of very few people in my graduating class who had jobs waiting for them upon graduation. Happy with my choice of majors or not, I was quite content with having a job. Three weeks after commencement, I became a member of the salaried population of adults. It felt good. It was yet another step in my continued mechanical and highly socially accepted progression through life.

Three weeks into the new job I knew I was in the wrong place because, the good feeling was gone and very shortly after that I was back at being unhappy and unengaged. Things that come easy tend not to be the things that satisfy, invigorate or inspire a person. Without a doubt, accepting the job offer was the continuation of my mechanical progression through life. Instead of working to alleviate my pain and work toward becoming an active, steering participant in the course-laying of my life, I choose to allow life to steer and place me where it would. Consequently, I submitted myself to going through the motions of working a job for which I felt unsuited and consequently hated. It was as though I was yet another incarcerated young Black man who, once again, was made a prisoner by his own willful mistake of not taking the time to think things through and not making good decisions in consideration of his unique design.

Possibly my comparison to incarceration is nothing more than the ranting and raving of an ungrateful and spoiled child, but what is prison other than a debilitating place of confinement. Walls are not necessary to confine a person. In fact prison is more a matter of the mind than the body. A free mind travels beyond walls. It goes outside the box and the truly free person seeks and takes direction from his free mind. I have never been so. I have never truly lived a free life.

I have lived a self-imposed, imprisoned life. I haven't had the faith or courage to step out and live in the realms beyond what I have considered comfortable. I have lived in the prison of familiarity and predictability. I have never, on my own, known how to live outside the box. I have only known how to follow acceptable paths that have had the appearance of being the right path or paths for me, and although replete with stress and pain, I have always been well acquainted with the terrain of the familiar and relatively safe paths. I have always been familiar with knowing how to follow the rules of good, clean, safe, expected and respectable living but very little, if anything, about living with passion, conviction and responsible risk. Although I had asked Christ into my life as a teenager, read my Bible and treated people with the love of Christ, I have never really felt that I was living a faith-based Christian life. The safe and fairly predictable life I have lived is largely by my own creation, not God's. I have followed the safe roadmap and where it has gotten me is a place where I have experienced an ever increasing dread of my life.

Gainfully employed, I was in an enviable position as thought by many people. I was years ahead of many who had graduated with me from high school and even college: whether a job is enjoyed or not, having one is no small thing. Struggling within myself, on several occasions I thought about quitting but on those same occasions I thought about how silly I would sound to my parents and family members trying to explain the logic of quitting a highly respected job making good, respectable money. I simply couldn't do it. So—on the job I remained: unhappy and more and more fractured from truly living the life God gave me.

I was a fish out of water and because of an inability to find the courage, conviction and direction to move myself toward a stream, river, lake or ocean suitable to my design, on the beach I remained, floundering and gasping for what I needed—the flowing currents of ponds unknown but nourishing. I must say, however, that God didn't completely relegate me to the life-sapping sands of the beach on which I floundered. God made it possible for me to meet and to become friends with Hector Santiago and he did so right after church one sunny, Sunday morning.

After morning service had ended I had a taste for some home fried chicken. I walked straight from the church to Willie's Wings. Willie's Wings was known for the best home fried chicken that wasn't fried at home. The place was always crowded, especially after church. As crowded as the place was I went anyway. There was no place to sit, but that didn't matter because, I was prepared to take my food out and eat it in the car on the way home. As things turned out, though, someone called to me as I was leaving with my food.

"Yo, if you're looking for a spot here's one." Much preferring to sit and eat at Willie's than to eat in my car I took the stranger up on his offer. Seated, I dug into my chicken and didn't come up for air until I felt eyes on me. Remaining face down, I turned my eyes up and to the right. The inviting stranger was staring at me. For several silent seconds we starred at each other until he broke the deadlock. Loudly, even attracting attention, he said, "You are one hungry Negro aren't you?" I stared at him in utter disbelief. Why I didn't remove myself from his presence is still a mystery to me. To this day I don't know why I stayed there.

Immediately following his rude outburst he laughed, smiled and introduced himself, "Hector Santiago." He extended his right hand for a hand shake but after staring at my greasy fingers he pulled his hand back and instead patted me, genuinely and gently, on the back. I remained staring at him in disbelief. With a confident grin on his face he asked, "So what's your name?"

I wiped my fingers and mumbled, "George Grey."

Smiling quite lightheartedly he spoke again, "Good meeting you. You know I wasn't trying to be disrespectful. I was just checking out how you were tearing into your chicken. I just had to watch the show. You know what I'm saying?" I couldn't shake my disbelief, so I just continued to stare at this crude, unpretentious stranger. "Hey, I know what it is to be hungry and finally get something to eat. I wasn't judging you I was just entertained." Bored, crazy or ignorant on several levels, my rude neighbor pointed his finger to my church across the street. Then he asked, " . . . that's your church?"

Far from feeling comfortable, I mumbled, "Yes," then convicted that I should take advantage of the opportunity to invite an apparent heathen to church, I lightened up a bit and continued. "Yes, that's my church. It's Middle Valley Missionary Baptist Church. The pastor is Henry Whitaker II."

Almost cutting me off, my rude friend broke in, "Yeah I know Reverend Whitaker. He baptized me."

Involuntarily I blurted out, "He what?"

Laughing at the look of surprise on my face he continued, "I know Reverend Whitaker. He baptized me. You don't know what to make of that do you? Well, it's true. I may be a loud mouth and I am a Black Puerto Rican but Reverend Whitaker baptized me. My mother's been a member of that church since before we were born." Sheepishly I apologized.

Within a few minutes from my apology we got to talking about the church, the community, politics, the economy and the military. He had recently completed his military duty and as coincidence would have it, he knew Rayford. He and Rayford went through boot camp together in Alabama and several months later, they both ended up stationed at the same base in Germany. Hector and Rayford were very similar. They both joined the military at the age of eighteen, they both had energized personalities and they both lived life somewhat by the seat of their pants. I got an early window into the depth of how Hector lived by the seat of his pants when he shared with me how he joined the military. Hector decided to join the military within moments of waking up one morning in his eighteenth year of life and within hours of those very same moments he walked down to the enlisting office and signed his life away to the United States military. Hearing Hector's story and feeling stimulated as a result, I couldn't help thinking about Rayford's impact on my life and the very real possibility that my life needed the inspirations of an uninhibited friend. Before parting ways from the chicken place, Hector and I exchanged telephone numbers and in subsequent weeks we became good friends.

One morning Hector and I decided to do some early morning bicycle riding. As we were casually riding along we were in conversation. The subject of God came up. Hector shared a story about a young minister he had met in Japan. He described the man as a Dr. King clone. Hearing his description I laughed and told him that one of my best friends is like that. As we continued riding I noticed that a deep, reflective expression had come over Hector's face.

"Yeah, Rev Clarence helped me out alot that day."

"Reverend Clarence?" My eyes opened wide. "You mean Clarence Davenport?"

"Yeah, you know him?"

"Know him? That's the friend I was telling you about." In total disbelief Hector and I just looked at each other with puzzled looks for several moments.

"Small world—huh?"

"Yeah, definitely—real small world." For the rest of the ride we continued our talk about God and Clarence.

Later that evening it dawned on me that Clarence had gone to Japan for some evangelical crusade right after we graduated from college. As much as it was a reality that Hector knew both of my closest friends, it was hard to believe. The likelihood of it all seemed unfathomable. As unimaginable as it was though, it left me with good feelings.

Over the course of a year and a few months, I did many things with Hector. His free style type of life provided an escape for me and experiential glimpses of a way of living that was very different from how I lived my life. With only having infrequent conversations with Rayford, Hector, in many respects, had become my substitute Rayford. He was brash, crass and impudent but somehow always enlightening—just like Rayford.

# CHAPTER 18

# A Wonderful Experience

One Wednesday evening, a year or so after meeting Hector, Hector called me at work. Having no idea of my earned vacation hours, my workload or anything else, Hector proposed the idea of going on a trip.

"Hey—let's go camping up in Conway, New Hampshire for a week; we'll leave mid-day tomorrow and come back a week later, next Thursday. I'm going back on active duty, but I have just over one week before I have to report in. So, what do you say?"

All I could mutter was, "huh?"

Hector repeated himself then added, "C'mon live a little." Hector reminded me of Rayford.

Before I knew it I heard, "Let's do it," come out of my mouth.

The next morning I got to work early and secured my spontaneous vacation plans with the boss. My place of work didn't require submittal of formal requests for time off. If an employee's direct manager approved time off, then all was well and in order. Despite the laid back culture at work towards vacation hours, I never felt comfortable taking off from work at non holiday times though. I believe it was because I didn't truly feel like a full member of the team, and that, I believe, was due to my personal point of frustration of simply being the wrong guy for the job. It was consequently awkward for me as I prepared to leave at 11am. Fortunately for me, though, at that hour of morning, the minds and attention of my co-workers were focused on their various lunch plans and menus. I left virtually unnoticed.

Once I was out of the building, in my car and driving out of the company's parking lot, a great burden lifted from me. I breathed deeply extinguishing the anxiety that had built up inside me. Looking in the rearview mirror I noticed a grin emerging on my face. Soon though, the grin left. After experiencing the burden free euphoria of being away from work, I, for the first time since agreeing to the camping trip, actually thought about the trip in concrete terms.

I said out loud, "What are you smoking? You agreed to leave for the trip at mid-day. It is now a little past 11:00am, you haven't packed, you don't know what to pack, you don't really know where you're going and you don't own a single stitch of camping equipment. What are you smoking?"

I got to my apartment at 11:30am. I was prepared to call Hector as soon as I got in my apartment to inform him about my recent brush with reality. I parked my car and began to walk to my second floor apartment. There, sitting at the top of the stairs was Hector.

"Amigo, what's up? Get your stuff and let's get going. We have a long way to go, so let's get out of here." I shook my head and informed Hector that I wasn't packed and didn't have any camping equipment. Hector stood up from the step and informed me that all I needed was a tooth brush, but if I wanted, I could bring tooth paste, a towel, a pair of shorts, trunks, deodorant and underwear. Regarding camping gear he informed me that he had a sleeping bag in the car for me. To give my mind time to process the information I stood for a moment or two trying to soak it all in.

In mild frustration Hector told me to open the door, "Grey, please, just open the door and get the things I told you to get. I really wanna be on the road by noon. I want to get in as much time as we can with the left-wing folks, and I mean way left, you know the quiet socialists, avant-garde intellectuals, tree-huggers and political independents. They've already started arguing and I want in."

Even more confused I asked, "I thought we were going camping?"

In comical impatience Hector replied in a thick Puerto Rican accent, "Man—you are so uptight. Lighten up bro, life is way too short." Friendly but indignant I collected the items Hector told me to get and at noon we were in his car, on our way to Conway, New Hampshire.

Once we got going, Hector yelled out, "World Fellowship, here we come!"

In turn, I sarcastically yelled out, "Yes, indeed—my favorite place!"

Responding to my sarcasm, Hector turned to me and said, "I knew you'd be happy." Immediately after turning his head back to face and concentrate on the road ahead, I turned and faced him.

I knew he saw me out of his right peripheral view, so continuing our little brotherly cat and mouse game, with as non-indulgent an expression and voice tone as I could muster, I flatly stated, "You know good and well I don't know anything about World Fellowship. So why don't you, right now, tell me what and where the heck it is."

Hector burst into laughter, "Grey, man, you're a nut, you know that?"

"Me? No, you're the nut."

Hector turned to me again then after returning his eyes to the road mumbled with his eye brows raised, "Hmmm . . . well at least I know what and where World Fellowship is. It kinda makes you wonder who the real nut is—huh?"

Clearly corrected but entertained by my reckless friend, I mumbled, "Just drive. Man—you're a pain in the butt. You make answering the simplest questions so difficult." In silence, Hector just grinned like a Cheshire cat.

The playful banter with Hector occurred as we passed the Nyack exit on I-287 and I-87 heading toward the Tappan Zee Bridge. As we drove onto the Tappan Zee Bridge, we were heading toward Westchester County. The view of and from the bridge was wonderful. Exiting the bridge, we continued on I-287, Cross Westchester Expressway, toward the New England Thruway. We were cruising right along and other than having been indirectly informed that our destination was World Fellowship, I had no idea where we were going. The exhilarating aspect, though, was that I didn't care.

To care is in the basic design of a human being. I wouldn't change that even if I could, but it seems that in our evolving society, caring is becoming alarmingly destructive. I know it was with me and I know many people who, as I, live day-to-day with dangerously high stress levels. We are caring about too many things—needless things and often times the things that stress us are due to situations in which we have consciously placed ourselves.

As we continued our drive, I thought about the manner in which I live. For a while I was looking out of the side, front passenger window, but then I looked ahead. Maybe subconsciously I was tired of seeing what we were passing and wanted to see what was up ahead, not yet approached, not yet passed—the always new horizon.

As I watched the road, I asked Hector a question, "Do you consider your life busy?"

"Busy?" Hector said with a pause, "Grey—my life is crazy busy."

"So do you consider yourself stressed?"

Pausing again before speaking Hector answered, "Na, I'm not stressed. I just got a full life, you know? Why, you asking?"

"I was just curious. I don't see how you live like you live. Sometimes I envy you. It's like you navigate without a compass, whereas I need the surety of one." I noticed Hector pausing again before speaking.

Then, once he was ready he spoke, "I think I know what you're trying to say Grey, but I don't think you know what a compass is. A compass points north right?" I refused to answer. The juvenile question had to be rhetorical. Hector continued, "Well, since it points north, then you know where north is and every other direction. Now all you have to do is choose what direction you want to go in and then follow the compass in that direction. What I'm saying is that the compass only tells you the direction. It doesn't tell you how the road is going to be, when to turn or how close or far you are from where you want to be. So I say you're wrong. I use a compass and I'm cool with it but I think you're the one who doesn't use a compass. You want a fully loaded, state-of-the-art, every second auto-updating life—GPS; my friend, that doesn't exist." What Hector said, stopped me in my tracks. I couldn't argue with him.

He wasn't finished though. He went on, "Grey, you want to be instructed to turn left at the corner, to stop at the cross street for 6.2 seconds then proceed only after the blue bird perches on your shoulder, but man, that's a sucker's life. You have to instruct yourself and stop expecting a good life to just fall out of the sky. Man, I'm not trying to be mean but you don't like ruffling feathers and shaking bushes or disturbing the status quo. You don't like making hard decisions; you just kinda bob up and down like a buoy. Think about it, though, Grey, by keeping the status quo how much peace or enjoyment do you end up with? I'm just saying man. Figure out what you want. Figure out what you really believe in and then make decisions that you're going to live by to make your life amount to what you want." After Hector had said that, the car went silent. Neither of us had any more to say. Quietly I sat thinking about what Hector had said and quietly Hector sat continuing driving to World Fellowship.

Finally we arrived at the Interstate 95 junction. We entered onto I-95 and drove north through Connecticut and up to New Hampshire. The Atlantic shoreline, the eastern seaboard, was an ever present temptation to exit the interstate and head for a public beach for a refreshing swim. We kept our focus, though, and maintained our course toward our destination. Air conditioner off and our windows down, the soothing salty air carried by the breeze off the ocean filled the car and fostered much lighter conversation topics than life compasses and GPS units.

Once we entered New Hampshire, Hector announced that we had to be at World Fellowship by 5:30pm. There was immediacy in his voice that concerned me. It almost seemed to be a point of stress. I kept quiet for as long as I could wondering if something was wrong.

When I could no longer keep my question inside I asked, "Why do we have to be at World Fellowship by 5:30? Is everything alright?"

Hector flatly responded, "As long as we get there by 5:30pm nothing more could be right. What's today?"

I answered, "Thursday."

"Do you know what that means?"

Obviously I didn't but I indulged Hector and answered, "No, what?" Looking over to me with wide eyes Hector unveiled the mystery.

"They cook out on the grill on Thursdays. It's the only day of the week that they serve any red meat. So, if we miss the cook out, we don't see any more beef for the next seven days." With as grim a look on my face as any person could have had, I turned to Hector.

"How about you stop talking and get us up there pronto." Hector smiled and like a man possessed, exited the freeway and navigated through a maze of non-tourist, local, mountain roads. How he knew where he was going was beyond me. As Hector dedicated his attention to the road, I sat in the front passenger seat wondering, once again, what I had gotten myself into.

I knew we were in good shape when we saw a sign for World Fellowship and turned onto the indicated road. Driving along the long road that followed, we passed cabins and lodges situated in the midst of woods before getting to the check-in building: which I soon came to know was Lloyd Lodge. Whatever else I had been looking at was immediately placed in the shadow of this building upon which my eyes had quickly become fixed. Lloyd Lodge was the main building at World Fellowship. It resembled a century-old New England inn, with a wraparound porch. It housed a conference room, dining hall and office. It was enormous.

Arranged on the vast porch floor was an array of couches and chairs whose appearance made me think of an outside living room: a very spacious and enjoyable, outside living room. At the time I was totally ignorant of the impassioned discourses and debates that took place on that very outdoor living room, but in the days that followed I became all too familiar. It seemed that topics avoided by many, for being too sensitive or even taboo were at the top of the World Fellowship list for intellectual promenades and insurgence.

Lloyd Lodge was a big wooden lodge, possessing a warm and cozy character. Warm and cozy as it was, Lloyd Lodge was quite rustic. One could say its accommodations were on the level with indoor camping. There were no rooms with private baths. Having earlier been led to believe by Hector, that we would be sleeping under the stars without the covering of a roof, I was all too relieved to be in the lodge. I'm sure some of the other guests and World Fellowship employees were entertained by the child-like giddiness I displayed at the check-in desk. Had they asked for an encore I would have delightfully obliged them, relieved that every morning for the next week, I would not be waking up with a dew-moistened face, head and sleeping bag, but rather with my normal dry pasty mouth and crusty eyes. This is what made me as happy as a child until Hector informed me that we would not be sleeping in Lloyd Lodge or in any other four-walled domicile, but rather in tents a short distance away from Lloyd Lodge. We were at the check-in desk simply for Hector to ask some questions about the two or three species of rattlesnakes at the camp and to pick up some bug spray and two tents; the lodge kept a few small tents for visitors like Hector and me, who arrived empty handed.

Pulverized by the talk of snakes, I took in a deep breath and let it out slowly. I was determined that I could and would do whatever Hector did. I managed to be happy, though, that we would at least be in tents. I believe I got the idea of sleeping directly under the stars from the fact that Hector never mentioned tents, only sleeping bags.

One rainy afternoon the New England inn styled lodge made for the perfect alternate location for an afternoon discourse. It was the porch, however, and not the inside living area that was chosen for the heated and well animated exchanges. The ideas shared were numerous. Some were more thought out than others but all, it seemed, stimulated me to think. I was engrossed in all the topics. No one, it seemed, totally agreed with anyone else. People with similar thoughts fought and argued as vehemently with each other as they did with those having totally opposing beliefs and ideas. While it seemed, though, that each guest knew what the issues, problems or solutions were, their command of my attention was only as long as while they spoke, for when those with different or opposing thoughts and beliefs spoke it was with equal surety and confidence.

I whispered, "Wow—if this is what occurs in the governing populations of countries then it's no wonder there isn't any shortage of wars and disputes within and among nations."

Hector heard me and in a matched whisper responded, "These people aren't afraid to ruffle feathers and shake bushes."

The discourse must have gone on for three hours but it seemed to occur in timelessness. I enjoyed it so much that I didn't notice the passage of time. Luckily for us all the food preparers knew what time it was and though the conversation could have gone on for several more hours it ended with a call to assemble for dinner.

We ate at long wooden boarding house styled tables. I knew not to expect any beef, we had that at 5:30 on Thursday and Hector had already explained the beef situation for the next six days, but bark off the tree was something quite unexpected and alarming. Of course the food wasn't literally tree bark but it was food served very close to the way it naturally grew. Everything was bland and as natural as possible. It was hard getting used to it at first but after a while it began to grow on me. I have a hunch that there was no over eating at the camp. I believe we ate to satisfy hunger and stopped once the hunger was gone. I'm sure the early years in America were like this.

Progressively in my week at World Fellowship, I felt that America should be brought back to this type of food consumption. It just made sense. The food was healthy and without a doubt it didn't entice overeating. It seemed to be the perfect way to eradicate America's problem of overeating and the consequence—obesity. As I discovered, however, this healthy way of eating was just as much fair game for those who attended World Fellowship to debate as any other topic.

As filled with challenging talk and discussion as World Fellowship is, it wasn't all debate and pontification. Recreation was also a part of the experience and thanks to mile-long Whitton Pond, which is nestled in the woods, swimming was at the top of Hector's and my list of recreational activities. Canoeing, row boating, and fishing were also available recreational activities. One morning, a few hours after breakfast while taking a stroll, Hector excitedly suggested that we go for a swim. In full agreement with the idea we headed to our tents, our domiciles for the week, to change into our swimming trunks. After donning them we headed to Whitton Pond.

Having been exposed to swimming at early ages, Hector and I both knew how to swim and loved it. Our shared love of swimming, however, had two very distinct expressions. My love of swimming was the sheer delight of being in the water, feeling its essence and enjoying the confidence of being able to manage and navigate through it. Hector's love of swimming, on the other hand, was the engagement of the battle between him and the water.

The way to the pond was wooded. Between the roots of the trees and rocks we paid careful attention to where we placed our feet. Soon we came to a break in the trees and just beyond us, after a sandy beach, lay Whitton Pond.

Hector yelled out, "Let's go!" He ran onto the sand and after throwing his towel down he dove into the water. About 100 feet from the beach a small deck was floating. Hector swam to the deck and as he swam, he managed to look behind and motion and call to me, "Come on!" I was still on the beach. I had every intention of getting in the water, even swimming to the deck, but before I did anything else my toes would begin the process of getting my body acquainted and acclimated to the temperature of the water: everything in its place and in order was my motto.

By the time I got in the water, Hector had already climbed onto the floating deck. Once my body was acclimated, I was ready. I casually walked further into the water and at the right time I pushed off and began my swim to the deck. I hadn't swum for a year. To my surprise I felt strong and well-conditioned, so much so that I smiled to myself. Having not really been paying attention to my proximity to the deck, I decided to take a look forward. Because my strokes felt really good, I estimated that I was pretty close. After catching sight of the deck I was puzzled. As good as my strokes were, surely, I must have somehow changed course and ended up swimming towards another and farther deck. I stopped swimming and began treading water to get my bearings. Looking around I realized that there was only one floating deck and upon it Hector was sitting.

The well-conditioned feeling that I had earlier experienced, suddenly left me. Muscle fatigue was now all that I was feeling and as I continued treading water, it worsened. I made it half the distance to the deck. I could either swim back to the beach or swim the rest of the distance to the deck. Feeling more of the effects of fatigue, I began thinking that for all practical purposes I was treading water in a bottomless body of water, for if I had stopped treading, there wouldn't be anything upon which to stand and preserve my life. I felt a twinge of anxiety.

To calm myself I spoke, "You can do this." Hector's back was facing me. He was evidently engrossed in something in the distance ignorant or unconcerned about my situation. I was actually happy that his attention was not on me, though. I have no short supply of pride.

Successfully calmed down, I began to wonder how I appeared to anyone who might be looking at me.

Becoming a bit paranoid I spoke once again to myself, "I hope nobody is looking at me thinking I'm weak or pitiful." With that I resumed my swim to the deck encouraging myself, "Look good. Look strong," as I swam. It seems a shame to admit these things, but I tend to care a great deal, and probably more than I should, about what others think of me. Since I'm being honest, though, I have to also admit that my pride to look good and strong is what overcame the utter fatigue I was experiencing and it was what enabled me to successfully make it to the deck where Hector was none the wiser of the ordeal I had overcome. He only knew that it took quite a while for me to arrive at the deck and felt no restraint in mentioning that fact to me.

On the deck, chest heaving, I laid out flat on my back. I don't know how long I lay there looking up at the sky trying to recover from the swim, but it seemed too soon when Hector began telling me that he was going to swim out to the Island. I told him that I'd be right behind him thinking, at first, that swimming to the island was some code indicating that he was heading back to the beach to talk to some girls or something reasonable like that. Instead, though, Hector dove into the water and began swimming in the opposite direction of the beach. Confused, I raised and twisted my upper body and head in his direction. Propped up on my elbow and lower arm I looked to see if I could determine where he was going. He was headed toward an island in the pond. I hadn't even noticed the island until that time. Before long I lost sight of him. I couldn't believe what Hector was doing. There was no way I was going to follow him. I simply didn't have the physical or mental stamina to even consider swimming to the island.

After getting my breathing under control and a healthy feeling back in my limbs, I lowered myself back into the water and returned to the beach. At the beach I comfortably sat, perfectly content looking at the water and feeling the breeze that came every few minutes. There were other people sitting on and enjoying the beach. So, with a few of them I shared light and enjoyable conversation.

Looking out onto the pond, taking pause from a conversation, I saw Hector and a woman, both still in the water, but walking towards the beach. They were apparently done with swimming, for the moment anyway. The woman was no spring chicken. I later found her exact age to be eighty one along with the fact that she too had also swum to the island and back. Was this some World Fellowship cult initiation that would leave me to return home alone while Hector remained at the compound to never taste processed sugar again and forever be a wanted man for going AWAL? It of course was not, but stranger things have happened.

Taking a seat on the beach I learned of the discipline and techniques needed to make the swim to the island from both Hector and Griselda, the name of the eighty one year old woman. She was one of the nicest people I have ever met. She was a native of Sweden and having a very thick accent, I had to concentrate on every word she spoke to understand what she was saying. Hector wasn't overly attentive to what she was saying. He would jump into the conversation at different times but took no real responsibility in its success. I on the other hand, due to my personality of wanting to make sure people are comfortable and feel that I value them and what they say, ended up being the one Griselda focused on every time she spoke. Had Hector worked a bit harder to assist in the conversation, I think the job of understanding what Griselda was saying could have at least been shared by the two of us, but I guess we are only who we are. Having no desires to miss lunch, we left the beach and headed for the dining area.

The days at World Fellowship were really enjoyable. Each day's passing was pretty much a combination of sitting, talking, eating and relaxing. World Fellowship was a place for quiet retreat and thought provoking exchanges. While at the camp, I discovered that Hector was a regular visitor to the camp. He knew just about everyone and just about everyone knew him. Consequently, in a few short days I knew just about everyone and was a member of the family. It was a good feeling to be a part of this culture of people. Generally, they all return year after year and for the most part during the same week.

When our week had come to an end I told Hector and everyone else how much I enjoyed myself, and as Hector and I gathered our modest belongings, I thought what a wonderful gift I had been given to have been able to experience a place where one is free to express himself freely in the company of others and a place full of opportunities from which to grow. We left around noon. I found it interesting that on the way up the rush was to arrive in time for the red meat at the barbeque, but leaving on Thursday at high noon, we had no regrets of missing out on the barbeque that would occur in just a few short hours. What a difference a week makes.

For most of the drive back, both Hector and I were quiet. I think because the previous seven days were my first at World Fellowship, and World Fellowship is so different, I wanted to be alone with my thoughts as I sorted through the varied experiences and people I met. Hector on the other hand, I believe, was pre-occupied with the changes his life would experience beginning the next day: his first day back in the military. He was probably thinking about some covert operation for which he was going to volunteer. Of course I had no clue of what Hector was thinking, but the lack of awkwardness in the silence was full proof that the quiet was what we each desired.

We got back late Thursday. Hector dropped me off at my apartment then headed to his. Early the next morning I was awakened by the telephone. It was Hector calling to say bye.

"I'll check you later Grey. I'm heading out to get processed and then to be deployed. Hang tough and do whatcha gotta do to make your life something you can smile at—later."

"Ok Hector you do the same and you be safe."

With a confident, "You know it," Hector hung up. After a relaxing weekend following a great time at World Fellowship, Monday arrived and I was back at the grind. I settled back into the normal routine of my life of being unhappy, but too afraid or without conviction or vision to do anything about it.

# CHAPTER 19

# Changing Horizons

A full year passed from my world Fellowship experience and another summer was upon me. I had started to gain a little weight so I decided to start running in the evenings after work. One evening after getting home from work and changing into my sweats the phone rang.

"Hello."

"Hey Grey, guess who?" It was Clarence. We hadn't talked in about six months and as far as seeing each other, the elapsed time was approaching the three year mark. It was good hearing from him and I'm sure he heard the joy in my voice.

"Hey Clarence, what's going on? Where are you?" It was as though I could feel him smiling through the phone.

"I'm in town. I'm at my mother's house. Are you up for a visit? I got somebody with me I want you to meet." I knew it had to be a woman he wanted me to meet. I could just feel it.

"Man, you caught me just in time. I was getting ready to go for a run but I can run anytime, so y'all come on over." Right after hearing, "We're on our way," I heard someone talking to Clarence in the background.

When he came back to our conversation he corrected himself, "Oh wait, we'll be there in thirty minutes; my mother wants me to run a quick errand for her." I assured him that I wouldn't go anywhere and before hanging up I gave him directions to my place.

After hanging up I decided to make some constructive use of my time before the arrival of my buddy and, by my assumption, his lady friend. I went outside to wash my car. Washing my car would not only allow me to get something constructively done, but it would also allow me to spot Clarence the minute he pulled up and to be able to direct him to the visitor parking spaces.

Just as I had finished the car Clarence arrived. I smiled to myself as my eyes confirmed my assumption. Sitting beside him in the front passenger seat was a young lady, with whom I was sure he was in a, more than just friends, relationship. Although Clarence had friends who were female, he had never had an exclusive girlfriend, boyfriend relationship. As I walked toward his car I simultaneously directed him to the visitor parking area. The closer I got to the car the more I found myself aware of a somewhat awkward feeling inside me. It was strange, but I ignored it. Reaching the car, I walked to the driver's side where Clarence had just stepped out. We shook hands with big smiles on our faces.

"You're looking good man," I told him.

"Thanks, but no better than you."

"True, true," I said with a smile as Clarence started walking over to the passenger side of his car. He went to open the door for his lady friend. By the time he got there, though, she had already stepped out. Clarence locked the car door then proceeded back to the side of the car where I was still standing appropriately waiting to meet his friend. With the three of us together, it was then time for the introductions.

"Grey, this is Sandra Peterson. Sandra this is the one and only, the illustrious George Grey." Meeting Sandra was awkward. I think anyone observing the greeting would agree that an adequate amount of acceptable pleasantries were exchanged but I think also that most observing eyes would agree that an unmistakable amount of awkwardness was present as well: an awkwardness I wasn't able to ignore. Whose fault it was, in all objectivity, I can't say. Some people when they first meet get off to smooth and wonderful starts. Others don't get along at first, but after enough time has passed, their personalities meld together. Still others, no matter how much time is spent together, never progress from uncomfortable politeness.

In the awkwardness, that I'm sure we were all feeling, Clarence and I ended up in small talk. I was trying to feel out the situation. After a while I invited them inside.

"Do you want to come inside?" Just after inviting them in, I had notice a negative mood change in Sandra. At first Clarence said yes, but as we began to walk toward my apartment though, Clarence changed his mind.

"Grey, on second thought, we're going to head out. I really came by for you and Sandra to meet. I'll call you later so we can catch up."

It was obvious Sandra's mood swing was the cause of Clarence's change of plans. I didn't know what was going on with her. I did know, though, that Clarence was handling the situation as best he could. They got back in the car. Clarence rolled his window down. After saying goodbye to him I bent down to see Sandra in the passenger's seat.

"Sandra, it was nice meeting you and I hope to see you again real soon." Sandra didn't say a single word of goodbye or any other common courtesy word of departure. At that point in the game I was no fan of Sandra Peterson, but I knew that since she was my buddy's current choice of girlfriend, I had to keep up a veneer of congeniality. Sandra, on the other hand had no apparent plans or desires to hide her feelings which seemed to resonate, "Get me out of here" from the core of her being. As I watched them drive off, I turned and went to my apartment. I was feeling a little emotionally empty inside. I headed to my kitchen. Maybe a little food could help things out.

A few hours later the phone rang.

"Hello."

"Yo—what's up Grey?" It was Clarence again. He seemed unexpectedly happy as if nothing had happened.

I paused before continuing then asked, "Hey—what's going on? Is everything ok with you and Sandra?"

With surprise in his voice he responded, ". . . with me and Sandra? Why do you ask that?" Trying to collect myself from my utter disbelief of what I was hearing, I offered some memory restoring information.

"Well Sandra was pretty unhappy when you left."

In pretty much the same upbeat manner in which he had called, Clarence communicated, "Oh that—man it's all good, Sandra just wanted to spend some time alone with me. She was around family all day and didn't want to spend any more time sitting around bored listening to another family member or even friend talk to me while she sat around trying to look interested." Considering this news I brightened up a bit.

"Oh that's what the deal was?"

"Yeah, that's what happened. Plus she's a spoiled little princess. I will say, though, that her mood change had something to do with you too. She didn't exactly feel genuine warmth and open arms from you."

Shocked, my voice elevated a bit, "What are you talking about? I greeted her very politely and even when I had clearly seen her mood change and you guys were getting ready to leave I told her how nice it was to have met her." Clarence was quiet. Had we been speaking in person he would have had an expression of disbelief on his face as he stared at me.

"Grey, I really hope you knew that you were lying between your teeth because Sandra and I sure did." Then I heard Clarence laugh.

Defensively I responded, "What are you talking about?"

With not an ounce of anger or frustration in his voice Clarence said, "Grey," then paused and continued, "Grey, you were clearly insulted. So for you to tell Sandra, it was nice meeting her and that you hoped to see her again real soon was nothing but a jab back at her. Since your words weren't sincere she would have preferred them to have not been spoken. So she acted as if they weren't. If you wanna get deep with this conversation, I'm cool with it, if you want to. If you don't that's cool too."

Off balanced and somewhat insulted, but mostly curious I told Clarence emphatically, "Yeah, let's get deep."

Taking a deep breath and then exhaling Clarence continued, "Sandra doesn't feel compelled to hide her feelings like we were taught. She wears her emotions on her sleeve. It's clear when she is: happy or sad, interested or not interested, enjoying herself or not enjoying herself, liking the company she is in or not liking it. She is very simple. With people like us, there is a very high risk of her being rude or discourteous. At the end of the day, however, lonely or loved, liked or hated, she is who she is and she accepts it. She reminds me of Rayford minus the charisma. If you genuinely make yourself emotionally available to her, she will respond genuinely in kind to you. It is a bit of a one way street in the early stages of knowing her."

Having listened closely to Clarence, my thoughts of Sandra had changed. I was less agitated by the circumstances of our first meeting. I was not, however, accepting of her style.

"I'm glad you explained Sandra's personality to me Clarence. I confess I had some negative feelings toward her: not so much now though. If I'm being honest, though, I don't see how you deal with the rudeness."

"Grey, the way I see it, we have to get along with people in this world. We have to be team players with those who are like us and with those who are not. We have to guard against burning bridges and biting any hand that is feeding us or might possibly be feeding us in the possible future. Each person's walk through life is his own. As long as a person is satisfied with his progress along the road and his manner of journeying, then what right does somebody else have to impose judgment? But I know what you're saying, believe me I do. In fighting for justice for the voiceless people I have noticed an arrogance of those in charge, those who regulate the direction, current, temperature, fish population and fishing rules of the main stream. They tell the rest of us how to: live, speak, respond, behave, think and socialize. Sandra, although often politically incorrect, swims to the ebb and flow of her own river."

It was late. I had to get to bed. I had work in the morning so I signed off the phone conversation with Clarence.

"Hey Clarence—good talk but now I've got to hang up. I'll catch up with you and Sandra over the weekend. I have to work tomorrow but I have a three day weekend. Talk to you later."

"Ok Grey you get some sleep. I'll see you later."

I fell asleep with Clarence's words busily moving around in my mind and oddly enough my experiences at World Fellowship joined the mental traffic.

The next day, Friday, Rayford called me at work. He was coming to town for the long weekend with a lady friend. The reason for the long weekend was the fact that the 4th of July was on Monday. The 4th of July—the celebration of a young country, newly freed, facing the vast horizon of freedom's opportunities, pains, joys, successes, failures, responsibilities and adjustments. How fitting it was that Rayford, Clarence and I would be together as young adults recently free from the authority of our parents' rules and having been actively pursuing our individual paths through life complete with girlfriends established along those very same paths. What the long weekend held for us was anyone's guess.

My long weekend was shorter than Rayford's and Clarence's long weekend. We all had Monday off but I was the only one who had to work on Friday. The end of my Friday work day seemed to take forever to arrive but eventually it did arrive and just as I powered off my computer and turned to leave my office, Rayford called. He was at his Parent's house and wanted me to come by as soon as I could.

Happy at the idea of seeing him after a couple of years, I told him, "I'll be right over."

"Ok—cool. My girl Frieda is with me and Clarence is here with Sandra, so hurry up." Something happened. My enthusiasm left and I had a small change of plans which I shared with Rayford.

"Rayford, tell you what, let me go home and change clothes first." I was fully aware that I was going to have to see Sandra over the weekend, but somehow the reality of it being upon me so quickly was unpleasant. If I could have had things my way, Clarence, Rayford and I would have spent Friday evening to ourselves to catch each other up on the news of our lives. Hearing my update, Rayford simply told me to hurry up. We hung up. I went home, changed cloths, picked up my girlfriend and drove to Rayford's mother's house.

When my girlfriend and I arrived, everyone was in good spirits. Rayford's mother was beside herself. She was glowing with having a house full of people and to express her joy she cooked a great meal and insisted that we eat in and not out at some restaurant. Rayford's father was also glowing. I believe being in the company of three young women inspired him to gather some of his army paraphernalia, including pictures, and to share some war stories of his courage on the battlefield. He was a good storyteller and by virtue of that fact, a nice mood was set.

The good moods transferred to the table where everyone enjoyed loud stirring conversation over great tasting home cooking. It was a good evening and it set the stage for an enjoyable weekend which culminated in a two car caravan to the location of what the television news had touted as the best place for that year's fireworks show.

Every time I have spent a 4th of July with Clarence and Rayford we have always ended up stuck in bumper to bumper traffic, catching only glimpses of the show whenever luck of a good position of our car afforded us with a view. The 4th of July celebration with our girlfriends was no different. We spent it in traffic catching only glimpses of the show. Past 4th of July celebrations with my two childhood friends, we never had a short supply of fun and laughter and we didn't have a shortage of fun and laughter that 4th of July either. Whatever Clarence, Rayford and I would do together, it was always about the company and not the event. The girlfriends experienced our brand of fun and enjoyed themselves: surprising even Sandra. Would I have rather chosen to have spent the time with solely my friends? I probably would have, but life was moving along and we were growing and changing. I had to be willing to accept change even if it wasn't my first choice. It was, after all, the 4th of July and Clarence, Rayford and I were like newly independent America. Change, uncertainty and lots of it were on the horizon for each of us, and I could see that we were each on a good course.

## CHAPTER 20

# Things Coming to Light

S omewhat oblivious to the presence of my two friends on my porch, I raised my head up and back against the backrest of my chair.

I began to think out loud, "What makes a good life? Is it a good paying job? Is it getting married and having a family? Is it not being selfish and giving to others?" I thought surely it was none of these because I had achieved these but didn't, as a consequence, regard my life a good life.

Finding interest in my questions, Rayford answered it in somewhat of a similar, thinking-out-loud, manner, "A good life," he said, "is doing your own thing with no regrets. You gather as much information as you can. You think about it. You twist and turn it and look at it from every angle you can think of and then you express yourself based on what you came up with."

At first I was impressed with Rayford's answer but then a question came to my mind and eventually out of my mouth, "Well, what happens if you end up not liking or even hating the manner in which you expressed yourself? I mean what happens if you have people depending on you and based on some purist manner of self-expression, you end up doing something or maybe even worse, doing and saying something that has a long lasting, severely, negative effect on them?" As if slapped suddenly across the face, Rayford became sullen. He closed his lips and bowed his head. He stared at the floor boards of my porch with a vulnerable intensity I had never before seen in him. For one brief moment I was confused at what had just occurred, but a moment later I realized what I had unintentionally done.

I inhaled, held my breath for a moment, and then slowly exhaled. Out of the corner of my right eye, over Rayford's bowed head, I caught a glimpse of Clarence discretely looking over to me. Clarence was aware of what had happened as well and in silence he communicated with facial gestures that I wasn't at fault. I knew I wasn't at fault but I still felt guilty. Guilt wasn't the only emotion I was feeling, though. As strange as it may sound, I was also feeling a warming degree of comfort. Over the past several years I had become the host and sole guest at my own little pity party. With mounting intensity, I was becoming more and more consumed with the depressing reality of my lack luster, dissatisfying, disappointing, passion-less and direction-void life. Witnessing Rayford's state let me know that maybe I wasn't the only one with deep personal regrets. The meaning behind the age-old adage "misery loves company" was the source of the awkwardly timed, selfish comfort I experienced.

Feeling that enough time had elapsed, I spoke, "You ok Rayford?"

"Yeah I'm good Grey. Hey, I didn't tell you guys. I got word that my daughter graduated with honors with a bachelor's degree in finance."

In a respectful, soft tone Clarence asked Rayford, "Why didn't you attend the graduation?"

Rayford, still vulnerable, trapped his bottom lip between his front top and bottom teeth for a moment then answered, "She didn't want me there."

Maintaining his respect for Rayford Clarence asked, "Your daughter told you that?"

Rayford breathed an artificial laugh followed by a clarification, "Naw Clarence, but you know, I mean if I was her I wouldn't want me to come. How would that look—me just showing up for her success? It would look like I was trying to ignore all the lost years and take some credit for her success or something."

Being an understanding person, Clarence let it go with simply saying, "Hey, you know you're my brother—right?" I guess the sentiment of Clarence's words of brotherhood hit the right spot because for the first time since I led Rayford to his painful memories, he looked up, turned to Clarence with a smile and gave him a fist bump.

Then he turned to me and still smiling said, "Yo," and offered one to me as well: an offer I apologetically obliged. There in the comfortable silence that followed, my mind traveled back in time to when Rayford announced his marriage.

Paula and I were in our first apartment. We had been married for eighteen months and Paula was pregnant with our first child. We had just come in from a date at the movies when the phone rang. It was Rayford. He was always an upbeat person, but that night he was beyond upbeat.

"Yo Grey wassup man? I got some news for your ears. You ready?"

Eager to hear his news I answered, "I'm all ears."

"Guess what your boy is fin ta do? That's how y'all said it in Atlanta right—fin ta?"

Jokingly I replied, "Uh yeah some folks, I guess, but if you don't tell me what's going on, guess who's 'fin ta' hang up and tend to his pregnant wife?"

With a fake disgust in his voice Rayford replied, "I can't believe you would say that. Man I don't even know if I still wanna tell you."

Knowing full well that he couldn't keep his news, Rayford broke the two second silence that followed his empty threat, "Okay, okay I'll tell you but first you gotta get Clarence on the line. I really wanna tell both of you. Oh wait. Did you ever get three-way calling? You know, you're kind of a tight brotha with the dollars. Last time we talked you said three-way calling was a waste of money. Did you get it? I told you to get it." Even though I had purchased three-way phone service due to the very conversation to which Rayford was alluding, I didn't want to give him the satisfaction of knowing he had influenced my purchase, so I owned up to having purchased the service but gave the credit to Paula.

Then I asked him, "Are you home?"

Rayford replied, "Naw, that's part of why I called."

Fighting the temptation to find out why he had called, I asked Rayford to give me the number of the phone from which he was calling. He gave me the number, we hung up and I called Clarence. Once I got Clarence on the line I called Rayford back linking the three of us in a three-way call. After Rayford and Clarence exchanged hello, I got to the business at hand.

"Ok Rayford, what's going on? Where are you and what's your news?"

Excited, Rayford blurted out, "The French Quarters in New Orleans, Louisiana and I'm about to tie the knot with Gloria. Oh snap, gotta go fellas. Gloria and I are next. I'll call you later. Wish me luck."

As crazy as it all was, Rayford's and Gloria's wedding in a French Quarter Chapel was the start of one of the most exciting marriages and friendships I had ever seen. They were great together until Gloria began to settle down and become less impulsive. Their relationship plummeted. It got really bad and many things were said that I'm sure both Rayford and Gloria would take back if they could.

When they divorced, Gloria was two months pregnant with a baby girl. I never knew the details of their split but one thing I knew for certain—Rayford had no relationship with his daughter and up until he was shaken up by what I had said, I never knew that his decision to leave his daughter and possibly even Gloria bothered him so deeply.

The news of Rayford's divorce hit Clarence harder than it hit me. The day after Rayford called with the news of his impulsive marriage, Clarence called me and shared that he and his wife, Rachel, prayed for Rayford and Gloria's marriage the night of Rayford's call. Rachel and Clarence married two years before Paula and I tied the knot. At that time Clarence had just become the pastor of a small church in Trenton, New Jersey. Among a host of other pastoral duties, Clarence was actively involved in marriage counseling for couples on the road to marriage, already married and those entertaining throwing in the towel on marriage. He hated divorce and hated even more the effect it had on any children that might be involved.

As I came out of the fog of reminiscing upon Rayford's marriage and divorce, Rayford mustered up the courage to further expose his feelings.

"You know Grey, one of the biggest difference between you and me is that you tell it and I hold it. Earlier today when you were talking about dying and your life not even amounting to a blip on the radar, I understood exactly what you were saying. Since, however, I don't make a habit of talking about those types of things or even really dealing with them, I answered you like things don't bother me but now I'm being real with you. Things bother me man. My life bothers me, but I just move on and hope for the best. One life to live—that's all we got. If I stop to wonder about bad decisions I've made I don't know if I'd be able to get going again. That's why I keep moving, hoping that I'll get better at this game called life."

Eyes wide open and almost in total disbelief at what I had just heard, the only word that came out of my mouth was, "Whoa."

Continuing, Rayford turned to Clarence, "I guess you're the only one who's found the key to a happy life Clarence."

"If you only knew," was how Clarence responded and then continued, "I think Rayford is right about one thing, though. Grey—you do tell it. When you're unhappy you get it out. I'm alot like Rayford. I keep things in but the difference between Rayford and me is that I deal with it on the inside or at least I try. I want answers. I want to fix what's wrong. You guys don't know the half of it. I'm an assistant minister at my church and I get pulled in so many directions and all of them seem to have one thing in common; they all pull me away from my home, from my family. I can't truly say that I'm satisfied with where my life is either. Man—I help alot of people, but can I be truly credited with praise if my house isn't in order? Rachel and I have some real issues and I can't say I have the best relationship with my kids either.

"My family life started getting stressed after Rachel and I had our third child. The small church I pastored fell apart for various reasons and I started a new chapter of my ministry life at The Savior's House where I am now."

At the mention of the mega church, Rayford was momentarily seized by its reputation and interrupted Clarence, "That is one huge church."

Allowing Rayford time to share other thoughts Clarence politely paused then recognizing when Rayford was done he continued, "You would think that because I was one of several assistant ministers that my position wouldn't be a family-compromising one, but things got hectic quick and got only worse with time. There are so many needy people at church and in the community and, while I'm aware of that, I'm also aware that my family suffers from my commitments.

"It seems pretty trivial when I hear myself talk about it, but I can't seem to find and live the solution. I'm trying to figure life out too guys. Where is center? Where is the point of balance? Wherever it is I believe that's where self-satisfaction lives. I know God is center, but as crazy as this sounds, I find myself struggling with truly getting to center and anchoring myself there." After hearing Clarence I was at a total loss, while at the same time feeling an even greater intensity of comfort.

# CHAPTER 21

# Enlightenment

As our day together came to an end, my two friends and I stood from our porch chairs and exchanged heartfelt words of goodbye and gestures of brotherly love. I remained on the porch as they walked to their cars. I waived to them as they drove off and remained there until the tail lights of their cars had faded into the distance. A sullen mood came over me. Instead of turning to enter my house I stood staring out into the night with my hands in my front pockets.

A faintly spoken, "Well," followed by a deep sigh left my lips. I was feeling empty. It was similar to the emptiness many people experience when a period of pleasurable, but momentary, life-interrupting activity comes to an end. The funeral of course was not pleasurable, but the gathering of my friends was a more than welcomed departure from the routine of my life.

As I turned to enter my house, just beyond the screen door was Paula. The sheer sight of her warmed my soul. I opened the screen door and walked inside. From the way she looked at me I knew she knew how I was feeling or simply had a sense of what I needed. Through the connection of our eyes, she was able to push the emptiness away into a corner. We stood just inside the threshold of the front door in silence looking at each other.

Looking up and placing her soft hand on my cheek she asked, "Are you ok?"

Softly I replied, "I am now." Paula closed and locked the main front door then took me by the hand and led me away from the door to our bedroom.

"Let's get you in the bed Mr. Grey." After unbuttoning my shirt she kissed me then softly told me to finish getting ready for bed.

In bed, I held Paula to my chest with my right arm possessively over her back. In silence we lay there. The left side of her face rested motionlessly against my chest. I felt the slow and deep rhythm of her breathing. As I enjoyed her stillness, the ghost like presence of sullenness returned to me.

I stared out into the darkness of my bedroom and whispered to myself, "Why is it so hard for me to find peace? Why is it so hard for me to find balance and happiness in my life?"

Groggy, Paula softly asked, "What?"

Realizing she had not completely fallen asleep I simply responded, "Shhhhh, you get some sleep. We'll talk tomorrow." I kissed her forehead and within seconds, evidenced by the totally uninhibited way in which her head then rested against my chest, she was fast asleep.

It seemed only a few short moments later that I noticed the light of morning chasing the blackness of night away. I suppose that somewhere between telling Paula to get some sleep and noticing that morning was dawning, I too had fallen asleep.

Somewhere during the time I was asleep Paula had repositioned herself to a fetal position with her back towards me. I rolled onto my right side to face her back. In that direction I was also facing the closed blinds which covered the large picture window in our bedroom. On display against the slightly illuminated blinds was the partial silhouette of Paula's body. Up and down I visually rode the darkened contour of the left half of her body. A part of me wanted to wake her while another part of me wanted her to continue her slumber. I struggled with myself over what course of action to take or not to take. With an agony experienced by the part of me that wanted to awaken her, I slowly slipped out of bed having decided to take the more gentlemanly and considerate course of action.

Before proceeding to the bathroom to take care of my normal morning bathroom rituals, I reconsidered my decision. I turned and gazed upon my sleeping beauty. Reconsidering once again, closed my eyes for strength then turned and walked to the bathroom.

Closing the door behind me I muttered comically, "And you say you can't make hard decisions?" I laughed as I put toothpaste on my toothbrush and began to brush away the staleness of morning from my breath and teeth.

After finishing my bathroom rituals I put my bathrobe on and went downstairs. It was 5 O'clock in the morning. The house was quiet. The kids and Paula wouldn't be getting up for at least another couple of hours to get ready for church. The house was mine. A little hungry, I grabbed a donut and a glass of milk and headed for the den. I settled into my Lazy Boy and sat back enjoying the quiet of early morning. My mind began playing back the events of the day before. The reality of the demise of my friend, Hector, rushed to the forefront of my mind. The reality of no longer having the occasion or option to see or talk to him was strange. Death is final. There are no do overs. When death arrives, whatever the deceased had done, not done, said or not said, it has all been recorded and tucked away with no chance of ever being updated. Death is just as final for family, friends and acquaintances of the deceased. There are, similarly, no do overs. What was done, not done, said or not said with respect to the deceased is all a matter of unchangeable record.

I don't know to what degree Hector was satisfied with his life. Hector never shared that part of himself with me, so I will never know, but yesterday, I came to know the deep inner feelings of Rayford and Clarence with respect to self-satisfaction. They have grave dissatisfactions with the current quality of their lives based on conscious decisions, actions, indecisions and inactions they have made and not made, respectively.

Sitting in my Lazy Boy, dreamlike memories of poignant things my friends have said to me over the years flooded and echoed in my mind:

*"Do whatcha gotta do. Every man rows his own boat."*

*"Man, alot of dudes would love to have your life."*

*"You want a fully loaded, state-of-the-art, every second auto-updating life-GPS; my friend, that doesn't exist."*

*"Grey, you want to be instructed to turn left at the corner, to stop at the cross street for 6.2 seconds then proceed only after the blue bird perches on your shoulder, but man, that's a sucker's life . . ."*

*"You have to make some hard decisions that don't come with guarantees."*

*"Hang tough and do whatcha gotta do to make your life something you can smile at."*

*"A good life is doing your own thing with no regrets."*

*"Where is center? Where is the point of balance? Wherever they are I believe that's where self-satisfaction lives."*

*"I know God is center but as crazy as this sounds I find myself struggling with truly finding center and anchoring myself there."*

Hearing these words again was like a whispered but trusted voice telling me that I have all I need to improve my life in the manner in which I live and perceive it. Breaking the quiet of my exclusive time with my thoughts, I heard rumblings coming from upstairs. I rose from my chair, washed my glass and went upstairs to join my family in getting ready for church.

Once we got to church and we were situated in our pews, I browsed the Sunday service program. My eye caught the sermon title, "The futility of lukewarm—Rev 3:16." When it was time for the sermon, the Pastor rose from his chair situated between his two assistant ministers. Without any introduction or ice breaker he went straight into his sermon.

"Gray is somewhat of an ugly color. It is neither black nor white and isn't usually a popular color of choice. It is often associated with dreary days and depressed spirits. Although one might argue that it lies between black and white, it is rarely, if ever, associated with balance. The color gray is on par with the state of being lukewarm. Lukewarm is neither cold nor hot and it is rarely a desired temperature. Some people will hate you in this world. Others will love you. Such feelings or behaviors to the average person are clear but someone with whom you have a gray or lukewarm relationship is almost nonexistent. Such a person can easily be overlooked and not missed if their presence is removed from you. Yes, gray and lukewarm are no place to be or to remain. Spiritually such a state will leave it's bearer in a no man's land: a place where frustration runs rampant and passion is fleeting; a place distant from God. Church family, I implore you. Embrace the Lord our God as a truly needed, desired and sought after life-giving and purpose-providing savior."

The Pastor went on and offered more elaborations and explanations of God's displeasure with the state of being lukewarm as expressed in Revelations 3:16. He shared that in a state of being neither hot nor cold, that God said that he would spew such from his lips.

My experience with the morning's sermon was one of feeling as if I were the sole inspiration for the sermon and as if the Pastor were preaching to me and me alone. The feeling was strange but at the same time it left me awkwardly comforted. I held onto every word he spoke. The depression, frustration and dissatisfaction I had been experiencing for the greater part of my adult life was due to a gray, lukewarm state of my spiritual life.

The world isn't as simple as black and white. There are many shades of gray but the gray shades of life are normal outcomes of our limited knowledge; we are not perfect and we do not know everything. The acceptance of the various gray shades of life, however, should not be confused with acceptance of living a passion-void, purpose less, lukewarm or gray life. A person should not travel through his life in a shade of gray. Non-lukewarm or non-gray living requires hard, purpose-directed, passion proving decision making. A lifestyle lived in shades of gray will only bring sorrow to the bearer for such a lifestyle lacks what is needed by every human being—a conviction of purpose and passion. A person, with desires and hopes of living a purpose driven, satisfying life must not be lukewarm. He must not live with a lack of conviction or at least without a direction toward his convictions.

I had my work cut out for me but following church service, I had an encouragement deep inside me. I had to get closer to God. I had to start trusting more areas of my life over to God. I had to stop getting so disappointed with my life and to begin realizing and understanding that I was on a journey that was not complete.

I knew I was on a journey with God. It started when I asked Christ to be my savior in my early teens. What I needed was a spiritual tune-up. God is the source of everything I'm lacking. God is center like Clarence said. God has distaste for lukewarm and gray, like the pastor preached, so gray and lukewarm can't represent center or balance. Growing a dependence on God is where I will find balance and center.

Over the course of my adult life, I have become a stranger to thoroughly feeling good about myself and where I am in life. I don't want this anymore. I'm tired of being spiritually between black and white. I want to be an obedient, grateful and faith-based, daring child of God. I want to break the shackles of fear. I've got to find out what God wants me to do and resolve to do it. I've got to become a true man—a brilliantly colored man of God who is far from lukewarm and who is far from gray.